老城市

OLD CITY

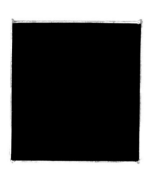

OLD XI'AN

Evening Glow of an Imperial City

Text by Jia Pingao

Text by: Jia Pingao
Photos by: China No.2 Historical Archive
Translatad by: Ma Wenqian
Edited by: Sun Haiyu

First edition 2001

Old Xi'an
   ─Evening Glow of an Imperial City

ISBN 7-119-02787-5

© Foreign Languages Press
Published by Foreign Languages Press
24 Baiwanzhuang Road, Beijing 100037, China
Home Page:http://www.flp.com.cn
E-mail Addresses: info@flp.com.cn
                 sales@flp.com.cn
Printed in the People's Republic of China

Foreword
Xi'an Is Xi'an Indeed

When I accepted the work of writing a book about the history of Xi'an, I was actually committed myself to a tough job. For one reason, I am not a native of Xi'an, though I have lived in the city for twenty-seven years, and can hardly give a thorough account of its past. Another reason is the scarcity of old photos of the old Xi'an that are available now, as opposed to piles of fading yellow photos available that one can collects to write a book about Beijing, Shanghai, Nanjing, Tianjin or Guangzhou. I went to one archive after another and raked through piles of files. I then ran to homes of connoisseurs and scrutinized at the antiques and paintings they had collected. What I obtained is only the stuff associated with the Xi'an Incident and the "Liberation of Xi'an", which are well known to Chinese. How can a book written on those events still be interesting?

Aren't there any photos of the past available about the old Xi'an? This raises a baffling question in one way or another. In effect the photographic information about Xi'an has never been in plenty. The old Xi'an without photographic annals just testifies to the fact of the city as being ancient. As is known to all, Xi'an was originally called Chang'an, the capital city of thirteen dynasties, particularly the Han and Tang dynasties when the city, as the heart of the country's politics, economy, military and culture, was famous for its magnificence and prosperity. As the Song and Yuan Dynasties came and passed and the capital seat was moved to the north, however, the popularity of Xi'an gradually faded.

By the third and fourth decades of the twentieth century, the ancient city had dwindled to the size of an ordinary county town of today in Shaanxi. Enclosed by the city walls built in the Ming Dynasty, the city, with an area only one tenth of the Tang's capital, embraced dirt roads and one-story stores and looked out into crop fields, trenches, mounds and swamps outside the city walls with the gates missing. At dawn when going out of town, one often saw wolves, pulling their long brushy tails, roam around between ridges in the fields. At that time concessions were granted to foreign countries in Beijing and Shanghai, in which life was heavily tainted in foreign nature, such as fashionable women wearing high-heeled shoes and carrying the small lady's handbag and men being dressed in the western-styled suit hung with the pocket watch and uttering sporadic foreign words like "mister".

In Xi'an, however, on the street corners, large patches of advertisements covered the walls about aphrodisiac medications, remedies for sexually transmitted diseases and ointments for treating headache and scalds, with a couple of Shanghai movie stars' photos sticking out at places. Popularly, matches were called the foreign fire, and the soap the foreign soda. Even a photo studio emerged called "Good Reputation." What a fashionable thing to do to take pictures in a photo studio! A popular saying went at that time that one's soul would be snatched away, if one walked into the studio to have a photo taken, and that one should make sure to have his whole body photographed, or he could never escape being killed. What the taking of photos really looked like remained a puzzle to ninety percent of the locals, who would only steal a couple peeps inside when stopping by and quickly moved on.

Because of the few small photo studios existing by that time, of which only government officials, war lords and rich people took advantage, my hope was dashed for using old photos to represent the folk culture of the city more than half a century ago. Moreover, the same reason brought me to the sharp distinction that parts Xi'an from other metropolises like Beijing, Shanghai and Guangzhou.

But Xi'an is not trivial in any sense. From any perspective of examining the past and present of China, its historical significance can hardly be ignored.

In speaking of Xi'an, the local people, any one of them you can stop on the street, would brag away about it: "Well, you want to know something about Xi'an. During the time when it was capital city of the Han Dynasty (206 - 220 B.C.) and the Tang Dynasty

(618-907), the northerners were dismissed as northern tribes and the southern areas the southern alien regions. Now the Sichuan Basin takes on the favorable name of 'nature's storehouse'. In fact the name was originally referred to our Xi'an which is located on the Central Shaanxi Plain. Xi'an is a point of the earth and the center of China. Situated around the city, Mount Hua is to its east, Mount Taibai to its west, the Qin Mountains to the south and the Wei River to the north. The city possesses the thickest loess in the country and the best preserved ancient fortifications in the world. Chang'an, the original name of Xi'an in history, means, in Chinese, long periods of order and stability. Was it ever flooded in the past? Never. Was it ripped by an earthquake? Never. Look at the Japs who rampantly invaded China. But their military march stopped just outside the city gates of Xi'an! It was said that Xi'an narrowly missed being selected as capital city of the new China in 1949. Think about those state heads who have visited China. Who would have passed on Xi'an as the third stop after Beijing and Shanghai on his itinerary for visiting the country? A tour around the country without paying a visit to Xi'an is only a fragmented visit to China at most!"

Such vanity and braggadocio might send people from other parts of the country laughing. But it is a reflection of the psyche that subconsciously but tenaciously gripped the mind of those from the declined family. When I started writing this book, the lack of old photos did not really bothered me, nor was I obsessed with the searching for a proper angle to begin with. I found it hard to specify the historical place of Xi'an. I often think a creature created on the earth should have its soul. A city is bound to have its soul. A big city like Xi'an, what does its soul look like?

In the color-fading thread-bound books, Shaanxi is short termed as Qin, an ancient tribe which lived in the distant regions in the Zhou Dynasty from the eleventh century B.C. to 771 B.C. With the tribe name of Yingshi, the people were skilled at horse-raising, and its first ancestor was granted the territory in which they lived for his meritorious horse-raising for Zhou's emperor Xiaowang. Originally this land was in Gansu instead of Shaanxi of today. This history complicates a problem of identity in that people from Shaanxi are not likely to call themselves natives of the province, because Shaanxi, actually, refers to the region west of the county of Shaan in Henan. During the Spring and Autumn Periods, the emperor Mugong of the Qin state (reigning in 659-621 B.C. and bringing his state into full development) expanded the territory to the west to embrace many regions of Shaanxi of today. The influence of the state grew more powerful in the following years, strengthening the long-sustained link of this region with Europe and other parts of Asia and scattering Qin's fame far and wide through the visitors of western tribes. Therefore neighboring countries called China Qin, a name translated in pronunciation that branches out to variations in ancient times such as Saini used by Persians, Xini by Hebrews and Zhina or Zhendan by ancient Hindus.

By the time the first emperor Shihuang (reigning in 246-210 B.C.)of the Qin state united the country, "driving the Huns out to the north and striking terror into the northern tribes, some of whom fled to as far as the present northern Europe ... and who then called China the Qin. This address was adopted and used by other European countries down to modern times." The transliteration of Qin is China. Chinese are also called the

Hans, the language used in China is Chinese, and a foreign scholar on the language and its culture is called Sinologist. In Japan the doctor on traditional Chinese medicine is called a doctor of Han medicine. Then how was the Han derived from history? Liu Bang, (a farmer, who led a rebellion of farmers against the rule of the Qin toward the end of the Qin Dynasty, then became the first emperor of the Han Dynasty, reigning in 206-194 B.C.) was granted a territory in central Shaanxi and the title of Prince Han, after the fall of the Qin Dynasty, by Xiang Yu, a senior military general of the Zhu state. A few years later Liu defeated Xiang and set up the Han Dynasty in Xi'an, who rose to the peak of development in the rule of the emperor Wudi (reigning in 140-86 B.C.).

The Silk Road was opened up, and merchants addressed themselves subjects of the Han Dynasty. The use of the Han was adopted by Western countries and handed down in history. Another spur of full social growth of the country came in the Tang Dynasty, when the Silk Road became a more prosperous medium of trade, and marine transportation and international exchange ushered in an era of unprecedented vigorousness. Foreigners called Chinese the Tang people, which has been used since then. Today the part of town in a large city, such New York and San Francisco in the U.S., Vancouver in Canada, Sao Paulo in Brazil, Melbourne in Australia, and Singapore, retains the name Chinatown, in which most overseas Chinese live.

In history the rest of the world got to know China by learning of Shaanxi and Xi'an, thus setting up the coordinate of studying the country. In my perspective, though I am not quite sure, one should concentrates on Beijing to understand China's modern civilization, and study Shanghai to know about China's contemporary civilization. But, to learn about the country's ancient civilization, focusing on Xi'an is the only way. It is probably true that Xi'an has no longer played the significant role as it did during the Qin, Han and Tang Dynasties. It started to decline in the eighteenth century and waned to a wretched state in the following centuries. It has now lagged behind many other provinces in industry and economy.

However, due to its long-time historical position, the city has preserved Chinese traditional culture in its true and multi-dimensional sense. (In Modern times Chinese tradition is often referred to things handed down from the Ming and Qing Dynasties, such as Chinese martial arts, lion dance with lanterns, mandarin gowns, Peking Opera, eating animal internal organs and drinking sorghum-and-maize-distilled spirits, which overseas Chinese like to showcase to the people in the foreign countries in which they live. But the things that best feature the Chinese nation are those that are handed down from the Han and Tang Dynasties.) With the tradition of a long history, Xi'an retains unique characteristics of boundlessness and profundity. It is this essence that sustains its existence, shrouds it with mystery, emits beams of glamour, and calls to the world for due attention.

CONTENTS

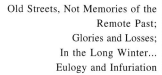

Chapter 1
Bricks of the Qin and
Tiles of the Han

The Mausoleum of the First Emperor of the Qin Dynasty. After the excavation of the clay figures of warriors and horses buried with the dead, the mystery of the mausoleum draws considerable public interest.

On the bank of Weihe River coolies are busy carrying goods.

Emperors Buried Here

It is in Shaanxi that emperors live and die. One old saying goes, "Scholars are from the south, generals are from the north and it is in Shaanxi that emperors live and die." I have toured around Jiangsu and Zhejiang. There in each county, I was shocked to see in the local library a long list of the names of those winning the title of Number One Scholar, from a few of them up to hundreds. But, in Shaanxi, over the long period of imperial examinations, only two men won this top title of learning, and even their fame was eclipsed with the allegation of winning through connections. Nevertheless, the deep yellowish land in Shaanxi is seen everywhere, such as the banks of the Yellow River

The tomb of Huangdi

A bird's-eye view of the woods surrounding the county and en-shrouding the tomb of Huangdi

The tomb of Baling of the Han emperor of Wendi

north of Xi'an that rise a couple of hundreds of meters high without a single rock the size of a fist. On the outskirts of Xi'an there are wells with a huge wheel erected on the platform. It takes two or even four persons holding the wheel with arms some while to pull up a bucket of water from the well.

On this thick yellowish culturally rich earth are the tombs of Huangdi, the first emperor, and the First Emperor of the Qin Dynasty, as well as those of the emperors of the Han and Tang Dynasties surrounding the city. They total more than thirty, including the Tomb of Changling of the Han emperor of Gaozu Liu Bang, the Tomb of Maoling of the Han emperor of Wudi Liu Che, the Tomb of Zhaoling of the Tang emperor of Taizong Li Shimin (reigning in 627-650), the Tombs of Qianling of the Tang emperor of Gaozong Li Zhi (reigning in 650-684) and his empress Wu Zetian.

Situated on the hillside, the Tang tombs are scattered over the counties of Pucheng, Fuping, Sanyuan, Jingyang, Liquan and QianXian on the Weibei Plain.

The seat of the Hongmen Banquet in Xinfengze, the county of Lingtong, in which it is said that Xiang Yu gives a banquet in honor of Liu Bang, with an intention of slaying the latter, who later sees through the scheme and makes an escape.

A distant view of Wuzhangyang, an ancient battlefield. The sounds of drums and bugles shot up into the sky as fierce battles were fought here in both ancient and modern times.

The Tomb of Maoling of the Han emperor of Wudi.

A Shaanxi boy wearing a short gown and a wrist-lace with a sparcely crew cut hair style.

Except the Tomb of Baling of the Han emperor of Wendi which is set up on the mounds, the rest of the tombs are large cone-shaped constructed tombs of earth on the mound of Xianyang resembling the Egyptian pyramid. Eroded in rain and human damage in the last two thousand years, the base of the tombs has dwindled and its top has been etched away. But the tombs look like mounds in distance. Yielding only crops and containing imperial tombs, the land of Shaanxi is scarce in mineral resources. The crops give people subsistence for living, and the imperial tombs have the symbol of throne buried in them. If a seed is planted in the earth and a plant grows up later, the symbol of throne is laid underground and an air of supremacy.

One Sunday fifteen years ago, I rode my bike along

A herd of sheep in a small grove, a sight exclusively obtained in the Shaaxi Plain in winter.

A village in the 1920s on the suburb of Xi'an against the background of a vast plain and the barren land of loess.

the bank of the Weihe River and came to a large cluster of tombs. Two of them were imperial tombs looking like two large hills, surrounded by seven mound-like tombs of officials, military generals and concubines. At twilight the sun edged its way down in the west, and the yellowish waves of the Weihe River rolled ahead, when the tombs were basked in the golden hue. I frenziedly pedaled my bike and finally dashed into the woods and fell off it. I broke into a laughter.

Farmer in this region live in the house made up of thick walls of yellowish earth. Built with four hard rafters, the four large rooms sit at the north side of the yard with some subordinate simply constructed rooms on the two flanks. Such house structures were lined neatly along the village alleys. Many people took advantage of the layout of the tombs and built their houses in the spaces among the tombs by digging a hole on top of the tomb, erecting an enclosing wall of earth and growing a few of crooked elms there. I figure the villages of today originally grew out of the living of those tomb keepers. The site of the imperial tomb, which was chosen for its high geomantic quality, may be a choice of omen for living, as opposed to the rundown state of these rural dwellings with no breath of thriving.

On the Central Shaanxi Plain, many people are the offspring of tomb keepers. To my mind, the county of Huangli, in which the tomb of Huangdi is situated, is probably the one that has the largest population of descendants of tomb keepers. Since quite a number of emperors lived and died in Shaanxi, many well known competent government officials and military generals serving the thrown emerged, too, on this land, only a few of them being from north and south China. Famous figures of Shaaxi origin appear in history in one generation after another, such as Hou Ji who teaches people to build houses, Da Yu who tames rivers, Zhang Qian who opens up the Silk Road, and Sima Qian who becomes the most outstanding historian in ancient

A yard with houses of mud brick

China.

In *A History of Twenty-five Dynasties and Periods,* more than one thousand people from Xi'an alone are listed up to the end of the Qing Dynasty (1644-1911), five percent of them being emperors. The majority of these recorded figures are capable government officials, valiant military generals, and loyal and righteous men. The rest are agronomists, astronomers, medical scientists, historians, exegetical scholars, literary writers, painters, calligraphers, musicians, performing artists, covering the three fields of learning, namely Confucianism, Taoism, Buddhism, and the complete nine schools of thoughts. Weiqu and Duqu, two places in the northern part of Xi'an, actually stem from the names of the two families of Wei and Du, from which forty prime ministers rose in history, plus hundreds of high-ranking government officials.

In the years that followed the Han and Tang Dynasties, the imperial reputation started to fade in Shaanxi. One folk story says Wu Zetian (wife of the emperor Gaozong of the Tang Dynasty, who becomes empress and reigns in 684-705) ordered in vain the peony to bloom in winter so she left Xi'an, and later the plant started to grow in Luoyang. Situated inside the city, the Large Pagoda of Wild Goose and the Qujiang Pond are traditionally compared to the imperial seal and red ink case. Now the former has survived but is leaning, and the latter has dried up. As the world entered the twentieth century, the southerners prevailed over, channeling the course of the country's development. Old Xi'an grew into oblivion for lack of well known names rivaling for national attention.

Cixi the Dowager re-
turns to Beijing

History in Official and Unofficial Biographies

In 1900 the Eight-Power Allied Forces invaded Beijing and Cixi the Dowager (1835-1908, who originally served the emperor Xianfeng and, after the emperor's death, became de facto ruler of the country) fled to Xi'an, nudging the city back to the seat of capital. The resumption of being capital brought no fame but infamy to the old city. In addition the death of Zhao Shuqiao during this upheaval saddened the residents of Xi'an.

Zhao Shuqiao lived in the Street of Sweet-water Well in the southwest of the city. Since I lived in the Street of Shuangrenfu, a neighboring street to the Street

The Wengcheng Well with a long history at the Western Gate of Xi'an

of Sweat-water Well, I struck up acquaintance with one descendant of Zhao and frequented his home, drinking and having tea over there. It is a large compound occupied by ten-odd households. But the winding path, leading to the inner yard and partitioned by brick walls and asphalt felts, did not conceal the luxury living the place once knew in the past, as shown in plenty of evidence, such as the pillars two arm-spans around, windows with diamond-shaped carving, and decorated tops of the walls. Sitting in a tiny room on the flank, which, dark and damp-floored with delicately-built wooden window frames raised, is his sole piece of property, I spotted, in faint visibility, a few pieces of furniture, chairs and wardrobes of padauk, feeling a strong sense of despair and regret.

Zhao Shuqiao was successful in his political career, first as head of the department of penalty then as director of the military council, the highest rank that the people from Xi'an had ever come up to. The Street of Sweat-water Well almost became the residential area of the Zhaos. Zhao escorted Cixi in fleeing Beijing to his hometown in the west. One of the terms that the Eight-Power Allied Forces put forth in the negotiations with the Qing government was a severe punishment on Gang Yi and Zhao Shuqiao, two major supporters of the Boxers. Since the former died on his flight to the west, the foreigners made sure to capture the latter. Cixi thought highly of Zhao for his talents and was

Government officials being executed during the Qing Dynaty

Some of the local people of Xi'an pose, who were "honored with the imperial meeting" in Cixi's flight from the foreign invasion. It is said that this snapshot was taken by a foreigner.

reluctant to see him killed. So she first removed him from office then had him sentenced to death with reprieve. However, the foreigners would not let him go, so Cixi changed the verdict by ordering the immediate execution of him so as to pacify the foreign powers. As the news went around in the city, people from all walks of life in Xi'an rose in petitioning for Zhao, and tens of thousands rallied at the Clock Tower. Cixi had to alleviate his punishment with "granting him the taking of his own life" so he could die in complete body. Physically strong at the age of 54 and expecting all the time that a decree for pardon would come from Cixi, Zho Shuqiao procrastinated in taking first the opium repeatedly and then the poison. His life lingered before he was smothered to death when he was tied to a wooden board and his face was covered with sheets of yellow paste paper sprinkled with distilled spirit from sorghum. After his death, the men of the family all ran for their own life, leaving the women on the family savings for living. As the family condition

Generals Zhang Xueliang and Yang Hucheng before the Xi'an Incident

kept running down, the property was sold piece by piece and dwindled from one street to a half and from half a street to the houses in three yards, until tens of years later when the descendant of Zhao Shuqiao, the man I knew, lived in the small room. It is said that Zhao warned his family members in the death bed with the words, "Never be government official." The story has never been proved, but none in Zhao's following generations has held the government portfolio. His offspring all live on skills of different trades.

The excited audience watching the Northwest Opera

During the time of Zhao's being sentenced to death, one woman received the title of "First-rank Lady by Imperial Mandate". She was a widow living at the Fort of Appeasement in Sanyuan. She was good-looking and confident in handling things. Her husband used to be the richest man in her home village but soon died of illness after her marriage. The villagers all thought she had to marry someone else and this family would fall from prosperity. However, she resolved to go

Zhang and Yang accompanying Chiang Kai-shek in reviewing the military troops right before the Xi'an Incident; behind Chiang, Zhang rides on a black horse and Yang on a white horse.

against conventions and managed to run family affairs of this large household in perfect order. When Cixi came to Xi'an for refuge, this lady, for her insight and resolution, donated a horse cart full of gold and silver to the imperial court. Cixi was so moved that she wanted to adopt her as her daughter.

The two stories, one of a government official and the other of a local woman, feature the unique life of the people from Xi'an blending tragedy with comedy in the late years of the Qing Dynasty.

A few decades later, another famous politician and a local man of remarkable talent emerged, Yang Hucheng and Niu Daolian. Yang Hucheng, a key figure involved

Yang Hucheng addressing the audience before the performance staged by the Tradition-transforming Society

Zhiyuan, Yang Hucheng's former residence in Xi'an and today's Museum of Yang Hucheng

in the Xi'an Incident, is abundantly documented in books and media. He was originally a local war-lord in the areas north of the Wei River. Though straightforward and valiant, he was by no means impudent and unrefined. In December, 1936, he, along with Zhang Xueliang, a military general of the Kuomingtang's troops, seized the opportunity of Chiang Kai-shek's coming to Xi'an for overseeing military operations against the Communists and held him in custody for stopping him from continuing with the civil war and urging him to join forces with the Communist Party in fighting the Japanese invaders. This is the world-shocking Xi'an Incident. I read a memoir written by one who was involved in the Xi'an Incident. It describes Yang as a man who, though little educated, had an extraordi-

The guarded Xian railway station on December
4, 1936, when Chiang Kai-shek, with his aide Qian
Dajun, arrived in Xi'an in the company of Zhang
Xueliang.

The Xijing Hotel in Xi'an, in which the high-ranking officials from Nanjing stayed. Before the Xi'an Incident, the place bustled with activity and the rickshaw drawers were busy with work.

The Zhongzheng Gate on the city wall of Xi'an with the model of a bomb displayed on the side and the slogans written on the wall that sound like an urge to Chiang Kai-shek to make an immediate decision for fighting against Japanese aggression.

The central building of Zhang Xueliang's residence, located in Jinjiaxiang Road, Xi'an, in which the negotiations took place during the Xi'an Incident

nary memory and could recall unmistakably minute details of an event that happened many years before. When he made a speech, the sheets bearing the text were folded around the corner in many ways. Only he himself knew the different ways of folding that hinted him what he should say next in the speech. However, he would never follow the text as soon as he took the floor.

From the photos available now of Zhang Xueliang and Yang Hucheng, we can see one of them look combatively capable and unrestrained and another massively awe-striking and reserved. Yang's facial features are typical of people from central Shaanxi, big head with a wide forehead, resembling, in one way or another, the unearthed clay figures of warriors from the tomb of the First Emperor of the Qin Dynasty. Their unique appearances and personalities are clearly

A charted train for Chiang Kai-shek during the Xi'an Incident

shown in the style of their residences preserved in Xi'an, one of them being a western architecture and another a structure of traditional courtyard.

Almost a contemporary of Yang Hucheng, Niu Daolian came from the county of Lantian on the outskirts of Xi'an and became a celebrity. The local people did not know him by Niu Daolian. But Niu the Scholar was a household name. By the time I came to Xi'an, Niu the Scholar had been dead long. But stories about him still went around among city residents, who often talked about him at tea stalls and the table on which mahjong was played. One of the stories says that in 1926 Liu Zhenhua, a warlord from Henan, led his troops in invading Xi'an and could not take the city after eight months of besieging. Then his soldiers started digging a tunnel.

The city residents knew the tunnel would eventually find its way inside the city but could not figure out

Yang Hucheng poses with officials from the press circles of Xi'an on May 2, 1937, on the send-off meeting for his overseas investigation journey

Yang Hucheng was forced to go on an overseas "investigation" tour after the Xi'an Incident. He (fourth left) posed with some of his friends before departure.

where its mouth would be. Therefore a big jar filled with water was set in a hole on each street or alley, and people were sent to stay by it day and night, watching for signs in the surface of the water and trying to pick up sounds. Then Niu the Scholar made a suggestion to the city government. He did not point out the whereabouts of the tunnel mouth but asked the city government to enlarge a pool, called the Lotus Pond, and draw more water from nearby places to make it a lake. The lake quickly formed with water waist-deep. One day the level of the lake water suddenly declined. It turned out that the mouth of the tunnel wound its way to the bottom of the lake and the tunnel was flooded and collapsed.

In Lantian, his hometown, there are more stories about Niu the Scholar's extraordinary skills. On a bright sunny day, he would leave home with an umbrella. Seeing this, the villagers all followed suit. The one that occasionally doubted and took chance was sure to be drenched in the rain. At one time, Yang Hucheng's political life was jeopardized. He sent for Niu the Scholar for advice, who was drinking in a tavern in the Stable Gate Street. Niu wore a long gown all year around. He usually came to the tavern, bought a cup of liquor, raised his head and drank it without sitting down. When Yang's bodyguard came to invite him, Niu the Scholar gave him a slip of paper, before being talked

Duqu, General Yang Hucheng's tomb, which is located on the south outskirts of Xi'an

to. The paper bore the words, "Appoint to important positions those men whose name carries the character 'Mountain.'" As the saying goes, "The dragon depends on clouds for prestige, while the tiger sticks around the mountain for power," Yang Hucheng followed his advice and used a man called Wang Yishan. Later Yang's career turned for better.

While Zhao Shuqiao and Yang Hucheng are two important figures in the modern history of Xi'an, the widow from the Fort of Appeasement and Niu the Scholar become legendary in the popular culture. The stories of Zhao Shuqiao and Yang Hucheng are treated in biographies, which often come in tragedy. Those of the widow from the Fort of Appeasement and Niu the Scholar are unofficial popular accounts, which are full of comic elements. We admire heroes and persons of outstanding accomplishment, but they often emerge in time of adversity. The majority of people lead a regular, uneventful life that revolves on laws of nature.

Merchants traveling on the ancient road winding outside Xi'an

圖南府安西

鳳翔府界

河南界

漢中府界

興安州界

湖廣界

The map of the south part of Xi'an kept in one of the noble mansions in the late Qing Dynasty

Indexes of the Famous

If we draw a geographical line, the area to the west of Xi'an is called the western region, and that to the east of Xi'an is called the eastern region. In comparison, the western region is interesting. In the east region, there is Mount Hua, and the western region there is Mount Taibai. Mount Hua is shaped on one single rock, hard, tall, straight, and precipitous,

A one-hundred-foot gorge in Mount Hua. Without the iron chain and footholds cut on the cliff, how could one climb up to the top?

The map of the north part of Xi'an kept in one of the noble mansions in the late Qing Dynasty

Shao Yuanchong and his wife pose for a snapshot in front of the tomb of Huo Qubing. In the Xi'an Incident, Shao was an official sent by Chiang kai-shek to stay in Xi'an. He was killed by snipes in the political event. This is the last photo the couple took in life.

like a mountain for men, to my mind, for its masculine features. Climbing Mount Hua is a hike in its true sense. Shrouded in mystery, Mount Taibai ranges long and wide with undulating hills, snow-capped all year around, like a mountain for women, in my imagination, for its feminine features.

The Museum of Clay Figures of Warrior guarding the tomb of the First Emperor of the Qin Dynasty is located in the eastern region. In the western region,

there is the Museum of the Stone Sculptures of Huo Qubing (a famous military general in the period of the emperor of Wudi in the West Han Dynasty). I told each of my friends coming to tour Xi'an from other parts of the country that, if you are a politician, you should go and visit the clay figures of warriors to show your broad vision, and, if you are an artist, you should go and visit the tomb of Huo Qubing to discover a feeling of wholeness. On the plain of central Shaanxi in winter, the persimmon tree looks like a shape combining huge, coarse stakes and small, fine twigs. The ancient Northwest Opera sounds like a perfect blend of the loud call by the male actor and the soft voice by the actress. All this makes crystal clear the kind of people this soil has nurtured.

If Zhao Shuqiao and Yang Hucheng are not considered as being successful in their political or military career, gifted literary writers have kept coming up in

The carved stones of horses stepping upon the Huns

one generation after another since the beginning of the twentieth century, such as Yu Youren, Wu Mi, Wang Ziyun, Zhao Wangyun, Shi Lu, Liu Qing ..., whose artistic contributions are quite enough for people from Shaanxi or Xi'an to feel proud of.

Yu Youren is widely considered as the top scholar. His image as a long-waving-whiskered man is everlasting. His talents are supernaturally endowed. To the populace, his accomplishments are achieved only for admiration but not for emulation. Many calligraphers, at home and abroad, try to learn his style of brush-writing but few come even closer to him in their attempt. In the

A photo of Weng Tonghe

Yu Youren (1879-1964) known for his long whiskers in the political circles in the early period of the Republic of China

A stone tablet with the imperial edict on it erected inside the Temple of Learning in Xi'an, on which the writing is composed and written by Zhao Shiyan. The temple becomes one of the important houses for keeping tablet inscriptions, in which almost all major stone tablets bearing the inscriptions of the Tang Dynasty are collected.

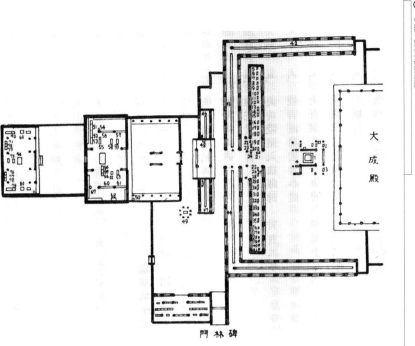

大
成
殿

碑 林 門

A plane of the For-
est of Steles of Xi'an

The Forest of
Steles of Xi'an

The Wild Goose Stele for Name Inscription inside the Temple of Grace in Xi'an

county of Changshu, Jiangsu, the hometown Weng Tonghe (a government official and a pace-setting calligrapher in the late Qing Dynasty), I saw a photo of Weng and was shocked at his resemblance in appearance to Yu Youren. His calligraphy was also well-known in his life time. After being removed from his position, he returned to his hometown. Visitors came thick and fast for learning his style of handwriting. Weng never granted their request. But Yu Youren never turned down anyone.

The people from Xi'an love Yu, not only for his writing but for his patriotism and maintenance of plain living for all his fame. He and Zhang Fang, a celebrity in the political and military circles of the day in Xi'an, traveled to every nook and corner in central Shaanxi in

The Many-pagoda Stele of Response from the Tang Dynasty, one of the stele in the Forest of Steles of Xi'an

The Imperial Platform Stele of Sarira from the Tang Dynasty, one the steles of the Forest of Steles of Xi'an

⇗

The Buddhist Stele of Mystery from the Tang Dynasty, one of the Forest of Steles of Xi'an

The inside of the Forest of Steles of Xi'an

The stele of the Sect of Daqinjing Popularized in China, which was originally erected in the Temple of Sage Worship and later moved into the Forest of Steles of Xi'an

search of stone tablets of the State of Wei of the late Han Dynasty and the Jin and Tang Dynasties. They often made every effort in obtaining one stone tablet by talking patiently to the owner and paying a high price with their own money. After quite a number of tablets were collected, they decided, through consultation, that the stone tablets of the State of Wei and the Jin Dynasty would go to Yu Youren, while Zhang Fang would keep those of the Tang Dynasty.

As a result, Yu shipped all the stone tablets he collected to the Temple of Learning in Xi'an, which has now become the internationally known Museum of Stone Tablets. Moreover, Zhang Fang moved those stone tablets from the Tang Dynasty to his hometown in

Zhang Fang

Henan and set up the "Store of the Tang Archives." As proved by the saying that the great man is created in heaven, two marvelous stones were discovered in Xi'an a couple of years ago, which caused a sensation in the circle of collection. One of them bears a true-to-

A sketch of Liu Qing

life head portrait of Mao Zedong. Another is a complete black stone that comes to light from the Qianjing River in the Sanyuan county, Yu Youren's hometown, and carries a handwriting tremendously resembling that of Yu Youren, attracting all his worshipping calligraphers of the city to take a look. The admirers bowed in front of it in reverence as if Yu himself were present.

Beside Yu Youren, credits for making important contributions to the protection and development of the ancient arts of Shaanxi should go to Wang Ziyun. Among the local people he is not well known. But his accomplishments are treated as master pieces in the fields of fine arts and archeology. In the 1930s-40s, he explored all the ancient tombs, shrines, grottos and caves in Shaanxi, searching, collecting and cataloging the cultural relics. A browse in his diary of investigation shows he led a group of people, at the wartime, trekking in barren mountains and living in deserted

A portrait of Wang Ziyun

Making rubbings becomes very popular among calligraphers. Here are two men in the picture making rubbings from the stone tablet at the tomb of Li Ji of the Tang Dynasty.

temples. They often went starved and drank nothing the whole day and had to dodge soldiers and bandits and fight against wolves. I once saw a photo showing him dressed in rags with disheveled hair, standing on a wooden rack and making rubbings from a stone tablet. He first discovered the tremendous artistic value of the carved stones in front of the tomb of Huo Qubing, and his craftsmanship of making a complete set of rubbings from these rounded stone figures is still unmatched today.

Renovation on temples has never ceased through thousands of years. Here the painting model is being produced on the carving of the Tower of Magnificence from the Tang Dynasty.

Shi Lu and Liu Qing are regarded as two remarkable talents. They went to Yanan in the 1940s and returned to Xi'an to pursue their artistic careers. Unique in character, they left behind many legendary tales of their life. In the mind of an outsider, people from Shaanxi are unrefined, including artists. The appearance of Shi Lu and Liu Qing testifies to this impression. Shi Lu wore the long hair and was slovenly dressed; Liu Qing had the head shaved and wore the Chinese-style jacket with buttons down the front. However, they were fervid worshippers of things foreign. Shi sang and danced beautifully and was good at fine arts of Western style. He even wrote some film scripts. Liu went further to master four foreign languages and read English newspapers all the time. The two men leave behind their master pieces that will become part of China's cultural

A stone figure of woman from the Tang Dynasty excavated at the railway station of Xi'an

relics and go on with the time.

I was born too late. Though living in the same city, I did not have chance to meet Yu Youren, Wang Ziyun, Shi Lu and Liu Qing. At night I often strolled out alone on the street, watching the crowds of people and traffic thin out and neon lights dim. The square-and-triangle-shaped single-story houses and high buildings were silhouetted against the dark light of the windless foggy night. Occasionally the music of the Northwest Opera drifted out of one house, when a crowd of people huddled together at the crossroad, playing Chinese chess. The glittering light of a cigarette dangled between the lips of an old man squatting at the pedestrian island at the center of the street. I was often lost in thought: how marvelous life is! Life goes on incessantly. But who built this city? Who first designed clothes, put buttons on the garment and invented cooking pots and bowls? We are better off with them but know nothing about our ancestors whose creations have made our life possible. Everyone knows Xi'an is a city of long civilization. But how did the city go through in the civilization? Cultural relics index history, while folk customs shape the soul of history. The nightly sky of today must have filled with the air of the intelligence and virtue of the great minds of ancient times.

A portrait of the young Yu Youren

A horse-fastened stake on the north side of the Wei River

A wretched sight of the entrance of the For- est of Steles of Xi'an in the 1930s

Splendid Relics

In 1923 Kang Youwei (1858-1927), leader of the Reformists of the late Qing Dynasty and later a royalist for restoration, arrived in Shaanxi at the invitation of the superintending commander of the Shaanxi military. An old well learned man, he received a great deal of acclaim and honor, when he made visits, gave lectures, went to banquets and wrote highly-valued pieces of calligraphy. On this trip to the province, he came in high spirits but left in disgrace. Here is the story. Kang Youwei went on a tour to the Temple of Sleeping Dragon in the vicinity of the Museum of the Forest of Steles of Xi'an. Knowing they were meeting Kang Youwei, the monks of the temple showed him *The Moraine Scriptures*, a book of immeasurable treasure that was kept in the temple. Admittedly Kang understood its value. So he took it back to his place with the excuse

瑤臺閬苑倚天半
白波青嶂非人間

天游老人

The old Kang Youwei and an antithetical couplet he wrote, signed in the name of "An Old Man of Extensive Travel."

for further reading. However, he soon left Shaanxi, taking the book along with him. When the news of his company's leaving arrived, the monks reported it to the headquarters of the superintending military, which immediately raised a commotion. Some local persons of renown expressed a firm demand for retrieving the treasure. But what kind of person Kang Youwei was! And how could they possibly humiliate him as a treacherous man by asking for the book in front of him? The monks chased him closely all the way to the Pass of Tong where they caught him. Blocking the way, they

The Temple of Sleeping Dragon in Xi'an, the largest temple of the Chan Sect of Buddhism in Changan, in which the famous the Song edition of the *Dazang Scriptures* is kept.

The strategic easterngate of the Pass of Tong

politely said to him that he was a well learned and knowl-
edgeable man, the only person that was aware of the
book's value, and it was shame that the book he took
was only part of the work of 1532 volumes and 6362
chapters. The book he took had been kept in the Temple
of Sleeping Dragon, while the rest was kept separately

in the Temple of Kaiyuan. If Kang really liked it, the monks promised to deliver to him the whole set of the work in a few days after they bound it. Kang Youwei laughed and returned the book to the monks.

Kang Youwei stole once. But he did not take it seriously that his misdeed became a butt of people's jokes over dinner. In the past sixty years, what has most enraged the people from Xi'an is the loss and damage of the relief sculptures of the six steeds on the Zhaoling Tomb of the Tang Emperor Taizong (reigning in 627-650). As six precious artistic relics, the relief sculptures are the six fine horses that the Tang emperor Taizong rode in life in fighting the enemy. The horses have their own names, Fenglu the Purple, Quanmao the Black-mouthed, Tele the Yellow, Wu the White-hoofed, Shifa the Red and Zhui the Black. Well known for its art of carving, the Tang Dynasty is further enhanced in reputation for embracing the style of power and vigor by these six pieces of art. They graphi-

Fenglu the Purple, one of the relief sculptures of the six steeds on the Zhaoling Tomb of the Tang Emperor Taizong, with the human figure of Qiu Xinggong standing in front of it. During the military campaign for attacking Luoyang, the emperor Taizong rode the horse, which was hit by a sniping arrow. The emperor sent for Qiu Xinggong for medical treatment on the horse. The relief sculpture of Fenglu the Purple is the only one, on which a human figure is created. In the early period of the Republic of China, it was criminally broken into a few chunks and shipped to the U.S.

The Pagoda of Tang Sanzang in Xi'an

The Zhaoling Tomb of the Tang Emperor Taizong is situated on the Mount Jiuxiao, 2200 meters high and 7.5 kilometers in width, north of the county of Liquan, Shaanxi. The tomb originally contained the relief sculptures of six famous steeds. Later two of them were stolen, and the rest are now kept in the provincial library in Xi'an.

cally present the six famous strong horses from the Western Regions in northwest China, three of them standing and the rest galloping.

Since the Ming (1368-1644) and Qing (1644-1911) Dynasties, no fine horse has ever been seen in Shaanxi. Those available on the plain of central Shaanxi are donkeys and mules, draft animals for plowing and carrying goods. Therefore people from Shaanxi highly valued the works of horses. But, one windy moonly night in 1936, an American ganged up with some profiteers of antique, stole two of the six horses, Fenglu the Purple and Quanmao the Black-mouthed, and broke and concealed the rest four. Immediately the people of Xi'an rose in hunting down the criminals and eventually retrieved the four horses in pieces. Today the relief sculptures of the four horses on display in the Forest of Steles of Xi'an are reproductions on the damaged forms.

Since the beginning of the twentieth century, historical relics have been unearthed in succession, each of them creating a stir at home and abroad. However, the stories behind the excavated items shine more brightly in complexity and wonderment. The discovery of the skulls of the Lantian ape men was achieved in the digging of a certain kind of rock powder, often made by local people in a gully for producing a remedy for injury. The discovery aroused the attention of scientists and led to the conclusion on its being the animal fossils of remote antiquity and the excavation construction. The pitches containing the clay figures of warriors and horses of the Qin Dynasty were discovered in Lintong, when the farmers used the ma-

A head painting of the clay warrior excavated from the tomb of the First Emperor of the Qin Dynasty

The Pagoda of Sui in Xi'an, which is undoubtedly among the most valuable in the city, containing tons of the historical relics from the prosperous Tang Dynasty.

The dilapidated stone framework at the Temple of Sage Worship in Xi'an

The Temple of Embracing Benevolence in Xi'an, in which monks came from India to preach the Buddhist scriptures in the early Sui Dynasty (581-618 B.C.) and which became one of the three largest places of translating the Buddhist scriptures. A stunning achievement was made when, in 809, the monks successfully calculated the meridian, a great contribution for coming generations.

A painting by Yan Ganyuan

chines to drill the motor-pumped wells and found some scraps of pottery. The underground court in the Temple of Buddhist Baptism emerged in the work of removing the debris after the temple collapsed.

I have lived in Xi'an for twenty-seven years and moved eight times. In each place where I lived, I saw historical relics unearthed whenever the digging was done for constructing the foundation of a new building, innumerable bricks from the Qin Dynasty and jars, tiles, copper coins and terracotta figurines from the Han Dynasty. Though they are certainly of high value on the national scale, almost each household possesses some of the items. The tiles of the Qin and Han Dynasties are often used by old ladies to impress decorative patterns in making steamed buns. Early in the 1990s, I stayed in a sanatorium south of the city. Outside the sanatorium was a field, strewn with piles of fragments of tile. The farmers cursed at the hindrance they posed to their plowing of the land. It turns out that the place used to be a shrine of the Tang Dynasty. Everyday in the afternoon I would saunter there and

The Temple of Cow Head in Xi'an

sift through the piles for tiles of worth. By the time of my recovery from sickness, I brought back home more than ten tiles with decorative patterns and characters.

Xi'an's richness in the historical relic gives rise to a great number of collectors. Among them Yan Ganyuan is probably the most successful. How many historical relics Yan collected is now impossible to pin down through research, because many of them were burned or lost during the Cultural Revolution. When order was restored to the country later, only one tenth of the loss returned. By the time I made a call on the Yans, the family already moved into a small yard in the alley of BaojiXiang at the Gate of South Yard. After many years passed, the host of the yard was now Yan Bingchu, an eighty-year-old skinny but capable man. He told me about the history of the family that spans ages, difficulty and hardship that collectors went through and the knowledge that concerns the determination, collection and preservation of the historical relics. I was spellbound. Later I noticed I was sitting on a chair of padauk, made in the Ming Dynasty, and holding in my hand a tea bowl of the Qing Dynasty. Seeing a container set beside the table look strange, like a feed basin for the cat, I made an inquiry, "What is it made of?" My host replied, "It is the well-tempered porcelain from the county of Yaozhou in the period of Qianlong (1736-1796). It was a sunny morning, the rays of sunlight coming in through

A chair from the Ming Dynasty

the window lattices, and some creatures flew around in the air. I picked up, from the wardrobe, a few works of painting and calligraphy by Shi Tao, Zhu Da, Zheng Banqiao (all three of them being celebrated painters of the Qing Dynasty) and Zhang Daqian (a noted contemporary painter). I was wondered by the artistic mastery they displayed. In a trance for a moment, I waved my hand to drive away an insect flying around in front of the Zhang Daqian's painting, only to know it was a honeybee painted in the picture by the painter. A laughter broke out among the people sitting around.

A horse-hastening stake

Then the old man said to me, "You're able to enjoy calligraphy and painting and don't profiteer. I'd like to sell to you that six-foot scroll of calligraphy by Zheng Banqiao for 5000 yuan, half its original price. Since we do not live far apart from one another, I can go to your place, if I miss it, and take a look." Unfortunately I was poor and stingy at that time. So I didn't take his offer. A few years later when I made another call to him, the old man died three months before. His grandson did not know me so I was shut outside the gate, frightened by the threatening barks of a dog as ferocious as a panther.

In Shaanxi there are plenty of historical museums. I visited the museum of bronze ware in Zhouyuan, the museum of bricks and pottery from the Qin Dynasty in Xianyang, the Forest of Steles in Xi'an, the Xi'an Museum of History for its pottery figurines of

The Tower of Receiving Auspice and Clock Watching was originally the residence of the Princess Changning of the Tang Dynasty, called the Shrine of Sight and Dragon, which contained a stature of Lao-tzu so as to adopt the present name. In the Ming Dynasty the Taoist Gao Jingkuan renovated it. In later years, the building was moved to the heart of Xi'an and became the Clock Tower of today.

The Dacheng Palace of the Temple of Learning in Xi'an. It is a shame that it was burned to ashes in the period of the Republic of China.

the Han Dynasty and frescoes of the Tang Dynasty, the museum at Northwest University for the tiles, and the museum at Shaanxi Normal University for the famous notes and paintings. One feels proud to be a native of Xi'an, having the opportunity for understanding the periods of a brilliant history and enjoying the heartbreaking and moving stories from each piece of art collected in the museums.

The Shrine of the
Revered Mr. Du Inxian

Northwest University in the 1930s

Chapter 2
A Shame for Anything of Flourishing

An old street in Xi'an with its residents and customs of primitiveness and simplicity

A Xi'an downtown map printed in 1933

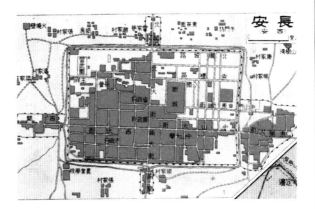

Old Streets, Not Memories of the Remote Past

I obtained a city map of Xi'an at the beginning of the twentieth century and found the names of those streets and alleys exactly the same as today. A closer look shows these names are typical of the metropolis in north China, such as the Road of Virtue, Gate of Training Ground, Street of Four Mansions, Market of Horse and Mule, Gate of Footstep, Lane of Affluence, Market of Bamboo and Palm-leaf, Street of Charcoal, Gate of Assistant Governor, Alley of Horse Farm, House of Two Nobles, Gate of North Yard, Road of Brightness, Road of Redpoll, Lane of Horse Track. It seems clear that these names originate in the Han and Tang Dynasties, probably no later than the Ming Dynasty.

Xi'an maintains its tradition of preserving history, tenaciously carrying on the language of antiquity to the vernacular of today. Many colloquial expressions,

A pier base at the gate of the Han City

The ancient city wall and a company of goods-carrying mules and horses

when written out, are elegant words. The Fu-styled poems of the Han Dynasty and poems of the Tang Dynasty, if articulated in the local dialect, are immaculately rhymed with perfect rhythm. The city has handed down ancient conventions. When a baby is born, eggs are supposed to be boiled, dyed in red and distributed to relatives and friends; when some one dies, the news should first be reported to the people concerned, and, to make sure, a slip of paper bearing the words "Pardon us for tardiness in making public" is to be posted on the wall outside the yard; the paper cutting practice for window decoration still goes on among many households; some people retain their interest in making flower-shaped dough ornaments; in a rainy day, one can still hear clatters of the cement shoes striking the pebble paved winding path.

In the past, the city walls went through a process of incessant renovations from the Han Dynasty to the Tang Dynasty and to the modern times. In 1980s when they were under another round of repair, I picked up a few intact old bricks and brought them home. I made an inkslab out of one of them and a relief sculpture on another, keeping the third just for enjoying its vigor-

A boulevard bustling with heavy traffic on the street outside the South Yard Gate of Xi'an

A scene of liveliness and excitement with crowds of people in front of the "Northwest Headquarters of Encircling and Suppressing the Communist Troops" at the South Yard Gate of Xian after the Xi'an Incident

A view of the streets at the South Yard Gate in Xi'an

ousness and simplicity. *A Lost City,* a novel I published a couple of years ago, offers stories related to real streets and alleys in Xi'an. Unfortunately the city proper later came under a large scale construction of transformation, which erased most of the old streets and alleys from the map, leaving behind only their names and distant and recent memories.

The place in which I have lived the longest in Xi'an is the South Yard Gate. This place is an agglomeration of the features of all the alleys and small streets. At that time, it was an area with bumpy roads and quadrangles, built with irregular sun-dried mud bricks, on top of which pinecone weeds grew and cats often came to sit and doze off. Over the yard wall were old cobweb-like electrical wires and iron wires stretching from one tree to another, on which quilts, garments and underwear hung for drying. The trees were scarred by the iron wire cutting deep into the trunk. On most of the lanes, there was only one water tap. In the morning and evening, residents would go there to fetch

A food stall runner
and the customers

A busy stall runner,
a richsha drawer and a
few children standing
motionless on the street
of Xi'an

A little boy wearing
the split pants, who just
wants to explore a little.

A little girl with a
cocking pigtail

water pushing the iron-wheeled wooden cart, whose clanks made people crazy. What most embarrassing came from the fact that the whole residential area had only one public latrine, in which filthy water trickled everywhere, and caution must be exercised in stepping around from one brick onto another.

When living at the South Yard Gate, many people ran into me and said to me, "Well, you live over there. It's a good place. Fifty years ago, it was the downtown!" In that residential area, some old men even uttered a jingle, peppered with foreign expressions, "Like Shanghai the South Yard Gate thrives with stores lining up the street; while silks and satins are sold in Sanyo, petroleum is in the hand of the American old company; time-honored FengXiang is known for its jewels and treasures, and Hengdeli makes the best house for watches and clocks; in addition, medicines go to "World" and "Five Continents" ....

The oldest of these old men, who recalled these words composed for the music, were in their early 80s. They were coolies pushing the water wagon at Wengcheng in the West Gate in the past. In the city

A vagrant fortune-teller with his birds

A well in Xi'an, a water source for the residents in the old times.

proper of Xi'an, the underground water is generally bitter or salty. Only the four large wells at Wengcheng in the West Gate yield clear and tasty water. One of the old man told me a story. Around 1939, he pushed a specially designed water wagon, something like a cart with a big wheel set in the middle and four water buckets hanging on the two sides. The bucket was 0.3 meters in diameter and 0.65 meters high with a small opening on the top for pouring in water and two ear-shaped handles on the sides for lifting.

Living was easy at the South Yard Gate. Except for the crematorium, one could find every living facility there. The name of the South Yard Gate was adopted in the fourteenth year of the emperor of Guangxu of the Qing Dynasty, when the Shaanxi headquarters of gar-

An advertisement for the Jewelry of Laobaocheng, on which a young lady and her little child are walking toward the store.

rison troops were moved from the Drum Tower to the south. Since the founding of the Republic of China, the place had been in succession the seat of the provincial legislature, provincial headquarters of the Kuomingtang and military field headquarters, always as Xi'an's political center.

In 1926 a shopping center was established at the Lane of Arrow west of the South Yard Gate, which included all the traditional stores of the city, the Lane of Flour, Five Spices, Corner of Mafang, Street of Zhengxue, Street of Guangji, Market of Bamboo and Palm Tree. The Market of Bamboo and Palm Tree had been the business center for selling bamboo articles since the Ming Dynasty. To the day, households there still sell items made of bamboo, such as the bed, chair, curtain, coop. The Waterlogged Lane was the work-

A spectacle of the opening of the show of circulation of domestic commodities at the Xi'an Museum of Education for Farmers

The Fans' Cured Meat in the 1990s

Today's "Spring Burgeoning" Steamed Buns Soaked in Gourd Head Mutton Soup

shop for painting, calligraphy, decoration, paper embroidery, farming tools, hardware, etc.

Some traditional snacks were sold at a few stores or stalls, fried flour with almonds, steamed pork, steamed cake with raisins, oatmeal gruel with dates, fried buckwheat flour. Keli Tailor was a special store for making and selling western style garments, in which the long-necked tailor with a big Adam's apple ranked first in the trade across northwest China and made garments for many celebrities. Beyond the Waterlogged Lance was the main business street, on which were the Fans' for cured meat, the Hans' for strung sausage, the Hes' for "Spring Burgeoning" steamed buns soaked with gourd head mutton, and the Wangs' for sheep blood sausage. One store sold the most orthodox spicy noodle of Xi'anXi'an, Shaanxi, while another one was famous for its standard sesame oil in central Shaanxi. At the Corner of Mafang, the shoe store, Peace and Blessing, ran business only for the shoes of famous brands. At the Street of Zhengxue there was a pen store which was known for making stone plates, engraving seals and making badges. A leather making mill, the earliest in the history of Xi'an, was situated on the paved road by the square. The "Modern Store" was run for face powder, vanishing cream, hair growing ointment and toilet water.

Located also there were the Shaanxi Library, founded in 1909, Books of Commerce, China Press, branch stores of the World, the Big Orient, and Beixing Press, and the Treasure Display Tower for displaying articles of tribute, which the Dowager Cixi brought to Xi'an in her retreat but did not take along with her in her return to Beijing. On the south Street of Guangji, there was Guangyu Drugstore, well known for making

A snapshot taken in front of the Treasure Display Tower

A photo of street fortune-telling

up the medicine for heatstroke and apricot pit eyedrops. Daren Drugstore and Zaolu Drugstore were even more well known for traditional Chinese medicine. Zaolu Drugstore was set up in the Tianqi period of the Ming Dynasty (1622), and the "Peikun Pills" it made was famous at home and abroad for its function of regulating menstruation, stabilizing the blood, enriching gas and protecting the fetus. At Spring Festival each year a lantern show was displayed in this place, sardine-packed with thousands of people, and the hubbub could be heard even way from the Clock Tower. At the three nights around the Lantern Festival, the lantern riddle fair was held stretching from the square on the main street to the Horse Farm Gate.

The fall of the South Yard Gate started after the

The west avenue under construction

The west avenue after the construction

founding of the Republic of China. In 1928 when Xi'an was enlarged to a city, the municipal government renamed the Mancheng District the New District and opened up two new roads running from east to west and from north to south. Later when the Longhai Railway reached Xi'an, the New District grew to be a new downtown. During the middle 1950s, businesses in private sectors were merged into joint ventures by the state and the individuals, and the handicraft industry became cooperatively run.

As stores and workshops merged, their owners shut down business, or found new employment or moved away. The prosperity that the South Yard Gate had in the past was gone for good. Today the South Yard Gate has put on a complete fresh appearance, high-rise buildings being seen everywhere, though its streets and alleys retain their original names. Despite

The South Yard Gate became part of Xi'an's downtown area at the beginning of the twentieth century, in which the three cliques gathered and stayed, the "Guangdong clique," "Beijing clique" and "Shaanxi clique," rivaling with one another.

Photos 1 and 2: At the beginning of the twentieth century people abstained from posing for the half-length picture, so they sat back straight to make sure of a full-length photographic image.

Photo 3 : The façade of the past White House Photo Studio;

Photo 4 : The façade of the past Dafang Photo Studio.

Set up in the 1940s and well equipped, Dafang Photo Studio was specialized in taking portraits, featuring a southern style of photography, and drew some political and military VIPs and social celebrities here for picture taking.

its fall in business, two stores selling traditional snacks started to thrive. The "Spring Burgeoning" Steamed Buns Soaked in Gourd Head Mutton Soup is now run in a tall building, and the Fans' Cured Meat is also expanded to a luxury compound with a two-bay shop front. Each day craving customers take taxi from all over the city to get there and stand in line in front of the restaurants, waiting to try the food.

A photo of two little brothers, taken in 1925. If they are still alive, the younger one should be quite old.

A photo of a mother with her kids taken in 1929. Today it would be a rare sight of a large family with the parents being proud of the number of children they raise.

A seven-and-a-half-ton road roller,
produced by the workers of Xi'an

The new-constructed west avenue

The clock Tower and Drum Tower were seen in downtown Xi'an in the past. But their view is blocked now by the large number of high-rise buildings. To see them one has to come closer.

Glories and Losses

The clock and drum towers are two fixtures in many cities. But the Xi'an versions of the towers stand out in magnificence across China. "The morning for the clock and the evening for the drum" has become a set phrase and been proved to be true here. To this day, crowds of people coming from other parts of the country gather, in the morning or evening, at the square of the Clock and Drum Towers in a hope to witness a team of people dressed in ancient costume ascend the towers to strike the clock and beat the drum, an occasion that takes one across ages to antiquity. The Clock Tower is situated at the heart of the city. The people from Xi'an embrace the dragon culture and believe the dragon lies with its head set in the place of Yuanshang,

The Clock Tower in the 1930s. The place becomes a downtown area today.

The city moat of
Xi'an

a village called Dragon Village just outside the North
Gate on the suburb of the city, while the Clock Tower
comes at the waist of the dragon.

Though the capital city for many dynasties in
history, Xi'an has an arid climate. It is extremely freezing in winter and hot in summer. There are actually two
seasons instead of four. No sooner has one taken off
the cotton-padded jacket than someone else is seen
on the street wearing the shirt. But such geographical
conditions have nurtured the "Wild Beast Troops" of

The street in front
of the Clock Tower in
the 1920s. As the street
was later widened, the
houses and stores that
used to line up the street
disappeared.

A bird's-eye view of Xi'an, the building in the distance being the Drum Tower

The horizontal board, originally hung on the south side of the Drum Clock, with the inscription of "A Place Rich in Great Men of Book Learning and Military Strategy," written by Zhang Kai, garrison commander in Shaanxi, in the imitation of the writing of the emperor Qianlong

Inspiring Anti-Japanese Slogans posted on the Clock Tower

The horizontal board, originally hung on the north side of the Drum Tower, with the inscription of "Sounds sent down from the skies," written probably by Li Yunkuan, a man from the county of Xianning

The Clock Tower after renovation, a building, like the Drum Tower, on the architecture of the Ming Dynasty

The Pass of Tong in Shaanxi, about seventy miles from Xi'an, which is called the east gate of central Shaanxi and used to draw crowds of merchants here for business from Shaanxi, Shanxi and Henan in history. Now this pass of military strategy becomes a rest place for travelers.

the First Emperor Yingzheng of the Qin Dynasty, the hottest pepper of Xi'anXi'an, the one-clove purple-skinned garlic, the strongest liquor "Xifeng", the Shaanxi dialect featuring loud, rigid, coarse and direct pronunciation, and the Northwest Opera derived on this pronunciation.

It is a popular scene in the restaurant, large or small, in which a group of people squatted on the stools, instead of sitting on them, with the pant legs pulled up and shirt sleeves rolled up, eating around a table loaded with "Xifeng" that goes with dishes of uncooked pepper, oily and appetite stimulating, mixed in salt, and some extra-large bowls of wide and belt-like noodles. With a purple-skinned garlic in hand, they enjoy the food and liquor to their content, the steam shooting off from the head, and, at the height of their enthusiasm, sing a song from the Northwest Opera. With weak capabilities of dealing with others, the people of Xi'an often run into trouble for their rigid, coarse and direct personality. But their dedication and perseverance pave the way to many inconceivable achieve-

A bird's-eye view from on top of the city wall over Xi'an, this ancient city

A homeless man is begging for food, but ladies and misses seldom dole out money, as shown in the expression in their eyes.

ments they succeed in obtaining. One case in point is the Xi'an besiegement that took place in the 1920s.

In the spring, 1926, the war-lord Liu Zhenhua, with the support of Wu Peifu, one of the Northern Warlords, and in collaboration with the Shanxi war-lord Yan Xishan, led an army of 100,000 in attacking Xi'an. It was strategically important to defend Xi'an in support of the Northern Expeditionary War waged by the Guangdong revolutionary government. But the defending troops in the city were less than 10,000, led by

A crowd of starved women and children at the charity house of porridge. They are supposed to pose for a snapshot as a memento. To a thoughtful mind, it is more for show than for giving relief.

A rally showing the unity of the Northeast and Northwest military troops, jointly held by Zhang Xueliang and Yang Hucheng shortly before the happening of the Xi'an Incident

Yang Hucheng, Li Hucheng and Wei Dingyi. One to ten, what considerable odds to fight against in protecting the city in eight months! Unable to capture the city, Li Zhenghua decided to besiege it, digging trenches and building earth walls, on which big guns were set up. He also had the 100,000 *mu* of wheat fields burned outside the city so as to sever the food supply of the people inside the city.

Threatened with the shortage of food, the soldiers and civilians in Xi'an dug edible wild herbs, peeled the bark, and ate dregs of oil and the bran. As the situation worsened, they started eating boiled leather belts and medicine. The dogs and horse were slaughtered, mice killed and sparrows captured, or even the human bodies were eaten, to quench the hunger. The following two paragraphs were written by some one who personally experienced the besieging of the city,

In 1926 Yang Hucheng, along with Li Huchen and Wei Dingyi, led the Shaanxi troops of the National Revolutionary Army in defending Xi'an for eight months, joined forces with the troops of the National Revolution Army that pledged resolution in Wuyuan and came down south, and overwhelmed the Song's troops of the Hebei war-lord army, giving a considerable support to the Northern Expedition. On November 28, 1930, people from all walks of life in Xi'an rallied in the Park of Revolution in commemoration of the fourth anniversary of the battle of defending Xi'an.

1. Human bodies were seen everywhere in the city. If they were not immediately removed from the street, starved dogs would rush over and devour them. Occa-

In January, 1931, the troops of the Seventeenth Route Army held a memorial rally in Xi'an for those who had laid down their life in all the battles against the enemies.

sionally some one was too weak to walk because of hunger and fell on the street, herds of dogs would glare at him with bared teeth.

2. On November 12, the blizzard raged and the gloomy sky hung heavily through the day and night. Streets were deserted and the death toll reached 2000. The following day I ventured out and saw numerous human bodies laid under the eaves and on the streets. Most of the dead were the male and old. The number of deaths among women and children was a lot smaller. Blue collar workers were hit the hardest by the toll in comparison with the smaller number of deaths among people in other professions. It is a general picture of the suffering of the people. I was shocked by the horrors, feeling I was landed in the infernal regions of the dead and devil.

Stricken by such considerable loss, the people of

Yang Hucheng poses with his wife and son. After the Xi'an Incident, Zhang Xueliang was reprimanded and put under house arrest by Chiang Kai-shek, and Yang Hucheng was forced, under pressure, to go overseas on a "tour of investigation."

The Xi'an Park of Revolution, situated in the northeast of the city and occupying a large area, is built to honor the memory of the military officers and soldiers who were killed in all the battles against the enemies in the past.

Xi'an hung on tenaciously for eight months and finally defeated Liu Zhenhua and succeeded in defending the city. In the aftermath of the war, a large pit was dug in one clearing on the Beixin Street, and about 10,000 human bodies were collected from all over the city and buried there. A museum was built at the tomb. In deep grief, Yang Hucheng wrote an elegiac couplet,

These men and women lived a glorious life and died a heroic death,
While central Shaanxi has achieved great glories and suffered huge losses.

One of the two leaders of the Xi'an Incident is Yang Hucheng. Undoubtedly, it is only in Xi'an that such event as Xi'an Besiegement could possibly take place, in which the military and civilians fought a fierce battle of eight months in defending the city with a loss of 40,000 lives. It is also only in Xi'an that such political event as the Xi'an Incident could break out, in which the people from Shaanxi, in the position of a local provincial army, took and put under arrest Chiang Kai-shek. I have been to the Lishan Hill in Lintong for many times and often wondered at the courage and intelligence that are aroused at the time of danger. So arrogant and self-assured as he was, Chiang Kai-shek, chairman of the National Military Commission of the Kuomingtang, sped up the hill, at the sound of the gun shots, clad in the sleeping robe and bare-footed, in the cold of the winter night, and crawled through a crack on the cliff.

But I admire more Yang Hucheng's courage, given his position and military strength. Anyone else would have kept quiet out of fear in front of Chiang. In addition Yang was "unrefined" in comparison with Zhang Xueliang. Zhang not only loved horse riding and hunting, he also took to flying the aircraft. By flying the aircraft, he once went over the Qinling Mountains to northern Sichuan to have a breakfast with someone there, then to Chongqing for business, to Luoyang to meet his friends, and finally back to Xi'an. What an unrestrained and style-pursuing character he is!

What type of living does Yang Hucheng lead to match Zhang in cooperation? Yang drank spirits, ate steamed buns soaked in mutton soup, sang roaringly the Northwest Opera, an honest and frank appearance. In pursuing his career, he counted on his admirable patriotism and Shaanxi style of gallantry. Never bending to power, he would rather rise in taking courageous steps at the risk of life. Stories go around that, during the Xi'an Incident, he once doubted Zhang Xueliang's faithfulness. He also demanded Chiang be executed. But, with the mediation of the Communist Party, he agreed to put the national interest before everything

In 1946 the Pavilion of Danger was built at the foot of the Rock of Tiger Stripes on the Lishan Hill. Later the name was changed to the Pavilion of Resurrection. Today it is called the Pavilion of Proposing with Military Force."

else and helped bring the Xi'an Incident to an end in peaceful terms. However, when the news came of Zhang Xueliang's leaving Xi'an in the escort with Chiang, he thumped his chest and stamped his feet, convinced that Zhang had taken a wrong step and he himself would be facing a dangerous situation. In the following days he shut himself inside the room, uttering no word at all.

On January 16, 1937, Yang Hucheng sent his representatives from Xi'an to Nanjing by air to call for the release of Zhang Xueliang.

Wu Mi, a celebrated scholar, once described the character of the people from Shaanxi: stubborn, unyielding, frank and direct. Truly described as they are, the people from Shaanxi are seldom represented in the central governments. Occasion-

Zhang Xueliang loves not only horse riding and hunting but also flying the aircraft.

Zhang Xueliang poses with his foreign friends around him before boarding the airplane.

Zhang Xueliang's handwriting regarding his leaving in the escort with Chiang Kaishek for Nanjing

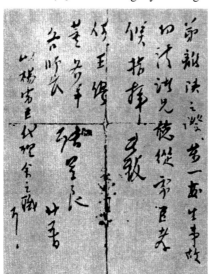

ally when someone is promoted to a high-ranking position, his tenure is usually short lived or ends in tragedy. During the besieging of Xi'an and the Xi'an Incident, Yang Hucheng had a coffin prepared for himself and made arrangements for his death to his subordinates and family members. During the battle, he ordered Chu Xiaobi, a noted gentleman who pushed for surrender, be executed. He also gave directive that no one be permitted to report about his own mother's critical condition at home, caused by the sickness, and any violation of his order would definitely ensure the penalty of execution.

At the rally of mobilization, he said, with tears in eyes, "Don't misunderstand me that I want you

After Chiang's capture, the aircraft, sent from Nanjing, lined up in the sky over Xian in threat.

The antiaircraft machine guns on the wall of the ancient city of Xi'an in close watch for possible raids from the airforce of Nanjing

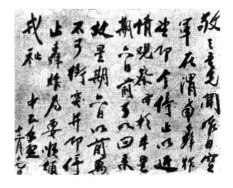

Chiang Kai-shek's letter to He Yingqin on the stopping of the bombing of Xi'an

夫君愛鑒：昨日紹西安之變，真急萬分。惟
先吾夫生生以身許國大公無私，先所作為無愧。
竟為自己個人權利，有怨即此一頁，才表是
以安列並此日為待吾。
先平日主張唯
兄以整個國家為重，故敢申來竭力盡頓，
深情國結願以發責處。此日主張此公意為
國之心豈為全國人民所認識耶目下吾
兄如以思此念相照望到
上帝賜吾
兄平日見難思託。
兄念神者
上帝賜吾兄平安歸來
外言為待將瑞書神祉不盡欲言等此布
謹並頌
臺安
妻美齡

Rena meets Zhang Xueliang.

After Chiang's capture, Madam Chiang asked Rena to forward a letter to Chiang. Rena was British living in Australia, who once worked as personal adviser to Zhang Xueliang and Chiang Kai-shek successively in the 1930s. In the letter she wrote the postscript, "A play inside a play," hinting the Nanjing central government had ulterior motives behind the attacking of Xi'an.

After Chiang's capture, the locals of Xi'an flock to see Chiang's personal airplane guarded by the Northwest troops.

to fight and die in the battle and I survive myself. I've made up my mind. On the day of the fall of this city, I will take my own life by the side of the Clock Tower to honor my loyalty and dedication to every one of you and the people!" He once gave a self-assessment about his life: I did three things in life, my killing of Li Zhen, a local tyrant in the county of Pucheng, when a young man of 18, so as to rid of the evil for the people, the successful defending of Xi'an in support of Sun Yat-sen's democratic revolution represented in Shaanxi, and the cooperation with Zhang Xueliang in launching the Xi'an Incident in an effort to stop the civil war and unit all forces in resistance against the Japanese aggression.

A book stall in the 1940s

In the Long Winter...

In the section of Xi'an close to the city wall, there is a market, called the Fair of Dew, or the Fair of Ghost. There business starts before dawn and closes at sunrise, on the selling and buying of used miscellaneous items and mainly for people of lower social status. The fair goes on to this day.

The gate of the Convent of Eight Immortals

In Xi'an there are two more spots that deserve visit, and I frequent them. One of them is the Convent of Eight Immortals, and the other the flea market on the south part of Road Red Finch. The former is a very popular Taoist shrine. On the first and fifteenth days each month by the lunar calendar, old ladies come over from the city, carrying their grandchild in the arms, to burn incense and kowtow inside the shrine. Because of this popular worship, business thrive on joss sticks, decorative paper, firecrackers, stall snacks and fortune-telling. Even antique shops mushroom to pack a whole street over there. I doubt the long-standing fair of antique and relic on the Street of Academic Learn-

The Convent of Eight Immortals is built on the ruins of the Temple of Celebration of the Tang Dynasty. It becomes a Taoist temple in the Song Dynasty (960-1279) and has sustained the religious worship through ages. Cixi the Dowager found refuge here on her west flight.

ing cannot expand its business for reasons, either being short of space or bad reputation caused by many fakes of its goods.

Anyway, the flea market on the south part of Road Red Finch is also known for antique business. I bought a pile of old photos in the Convent of Eight Immortals and a dozen of unsigned sketches. I was overjoyed by the haul of the photos on the relief work during the Xi'an's famine of 1929, particularly those horrible pictures showing the dying people in starvation on the street. The sketches are done by an anonymous painter about true life on the street. I was really delighted by the windfall of these materials on the Xi'an at the turn of the twentieth century.

In 1929 Shaanxi was ravaged by a drought, exceptionally severe in the history of China and the world. According to the data sent to the Nanjing central government, two millions died of hunger in the province, another two millions were left homeless, and eight millions lived on bark, weed roots and Guanyin earth. The Nanjing central government established the national board of relief and sent a delegation of investigation to Shaanxi. Looking at these photos and materials, I am upset to talk about this part of the history. People from Xi'an have avoided the mentioning of two things. One of them is the "going out of the YuXiang Gate." The YuXiang Gate was struck through the city wall by Feng YuXiang, who led his troops in rescuing Xi'an from the besiegement, and later became the execution ground of the Kuomingtang's governments in Xi'an in the 1940s. The other taboo is the talk of the drought of 1929.

The Xi'an besiegement of 1927 and the famine of 1929 sapped Xi'an devastatingly, causing its lag further behind from the concept of modernity. In the fol-

A little beggar on the street of Xi'an in 1929 in the severe drought

In May, 1927, Feng Yuxiang took the position of commander-in-chief of the Second Corps of the National Revolutionary Army in Xi'an. He won wide acclaim for the uniform he wore.

lowing ten years, it struggled in recovery and barely regained its former vitality before being stunned by the rapid growth of Beijing, Shanghai, Nanjing and Guangzhou. Over here the city was still a sight of provinciality, truthfully delineated in the sketches I bought on the flea market on the south part of Road Red Finch. I have two friends who come of wealthy stock in Xi'an. One of them said that in his early years he moved around town by car or the sedan chair, followed by four bodyguards. One of the notorious "ten rascal masters", he played table gambles, took opium, leered at prostitutes at the House of Green and Red and rioted in restaurants, smashing tables and chairs.

Liu Zhenhua, head of the Zhensong troops and a member of the Alliance Society

"But later I turned revolutionary," he raised his voice. People started to take to streets in marches against the starvation and civil war. Each time he heard a disturbance outside, he would dash to the street. But when his father was at home, he feared and stayed quiet indoors. In the afternoon his father had the habit of first having tea after the nap then practicing the sword dance, to keep fit, in the back yard with his recently married concubine. Each time the honk of the car was heard outside the house, his father put on his formal hat and walked out. Then he would pick up the triangle-shaped flag hidden in the corner of the bedroom and speed out.

Another friend of mine is a lady, younger than the previous man. She said her mother was from Shanghai

The façade of a brothel

and married to his father when he did business in Shanghai. Her father had conventional ways of disciplining his children. He required her elder sister smile without showing teeth and walk without flapping the skirt. He even had a little bell sewn on the hem of her skirt, and would scold her whenever she moved too fast and caused the bell to ring. Her mother was educated in foreign culture, good at writing poems, painting and, particularly, playing piano. She had the daily routine of going to the movie theater to watch movies. Young couples are seldom able to live without wrangles. Their marriage ended in divorce. "Look at this Chinese ancient dulcimer!" She moved out the music instrument. It was once used by her mother. Her mother left her when she was one and a half but never regretted for her decision of abandoning her. It is said that her mother married a financier and settled down in Hong Kong. Each family has its own problems to wrestle with.

In effect, stories about the rich and influential in Xi'an are relatively less known. Most of the city dwellers were busy with their work to make a living. Every

A four-wheeled animal-drawn cart at the beginning of the twentieth century

morning and evening the stench from the water that ran day and night around the city was blown to each corner across the city. In summer in particular, the odor stunk and lingered long in the air before dispersing. The perfume satchel was a must that women and young ladies of some social position would carry when going out on the street. In the area just inside the south gate, there was no building higher than the city wall. On top of the embrasured watchtower over the city gate, flocks of crows perched and smeared the bricks and pillars with white droppings. As soon as it got dark, they began cawing and the disturbance kept on for the night.

But the owls were creepier birds, who, like clay figures, squatted, during the day, on the watchtower and the ridges or the branches of elms along the city moat. No one dared to hit them. It was said that one incurred trouble to himself by hitting them. The appropriate treatment to them on an encounter was to throw up a few spits in the air toward them. Their caws at night struck a frightening note, when people were convinced that some one died in one of the lanes or streets the following day. Unmistakably the family of the deceased would hang paper sticks on the lintel of the gate, set up a mourning shed in the yard and hire a band to play music all through the night.

If the deceased was an adult, the white coffin containing the body, in two or three days, was carried on a

People say girls from Xi'an are pretty, because of their imperial descent. I think it is true.

wooden flatbed, in the company of wailing filial children and grandchildren, to the field outside of the city and buried there. If a baby less than one years old died, it was wrapped in a bundle of rags or weeds, set in a bamboo basket and left outside the door to be picked up by the "idler", who got paid for taking it to the field outside the city and bury it there. Today there is a popular expression in Xi'an, "idler", which refers to the unemployed street wanderer. However, "idler" originates in the trade, in which a bareheaded man, wearing a pair of white-soled, black-and-wide-uppered shoes and carrying a spade on the shoulder, was engaged in collecting and burying dead babies.

According to historical records, it was freezing in winter in Xi'an before the 1930s. It usually started snowing at the beginning of October by the lunar calendar, and the streets were covered with the snow

The Muslim children standing in front of the stone tablets inside a mosque.

one foot deep. Throughout the winter, the ground was ripped in cracks in coldness, bricks and tiles became softened, and half-meter-long icicles hung under the eaves. It was popular to wear the long overcoat lined with the sheep's wool or dog's fur, ear covers, and high-bodied cotton-padded shoes. People of lower classes had to do outside manual work, so the gloves were needed. But the glove only covered the wrist and back of the hand, leaving the fingers bare. People from rich families stayed at home, drinking. The wine was put in a bronze pot and kept warm over a

Coolies spend their night this way: drink tea, keep warm and have a chat.

brazier.

As early as in September people began preparing firewood, coal and charcoal for cooking and heating in the winter. The Alley of Virtue and Fortune on the east side at the South Yard Gate was the largest charcoal market. The charcoal workers usually had to work there long days and many months. They were old men, gray haired, who came down from the Southern Hill. But they could not afford the use of charcoal for keeping warm themselves. They often burned eggplant stalks

Early in winter, people from Xi'an shoulder the coal back home to heat up the bed for keeping warm.

and boiled the water with pepper and then steeped the hands and feet in it for alleviating the chilblains and cuts. Nearly in each quadrangle a pile of bundles of firewood was set on the steps of the house. On the street people hailed one another first with the sentence, "Did you have your dinner?" then with the sentence, "Have you got your stove coated with clay?" On the market some workers specialized in coating the stove with clay. They coated with clay the wall both inside and outside of the square gasoline pail made of galvanized iron. A stove such fixed could be heated with coal disks and charcoal. Fire could be ignited over the brazier.

Other heating facilities include the large-pronged stove and the sleeve stove, all made of silver-like copper-nickel alloy and covered with carved designs on them. The heatable brick bed was kept in wealthy and poor households alike. The only difference lies in the thick cotton-padded mattress or the felt pad spread over the bed in the rich family. In the poor family the bed was usually rimmed with a long shining wooden piece of cypress. When a friend or relative arrived, he was invited to take off the shoes and sit on the bed. The host would call someone loudly, "Go and buy some Yizi to heat the bed warmer!" Yizi is dried horse dung, or firewood dreg, and sold in stores. If the bed was still not warm enough, a "Hot Lady" would be stuck into the covering quilt, a flat round hot water container for keeping warm. One stone lion or tiger was certainly set on one corner of the bed. If the visitor came with a little child, a string of rope would be tied around the waist of the adult, while the other end of the string was fastened on the stone lion. Then the adult could be free to talk to the host without watching the child.

On a warm day when the sun came through, groups of people would huddle around the foot of the wall along the street. Wealthy people, clad in long gowns and mandarin jackets, sauntered along the street, the snowwhite fine lamb hair visibly

A stone lion at Yulin

The horse-drawn carriage is for passenger service only. It is the most popular transportation in Xi'an in the 1920s-30s.

curving around the collarband, cuff and the edge of the long gown. Someone of style wore a long and wide scarf, one end of it hanging across the front of the chest and the other end dangling behind across the back. Store assistants stood behind the counter, stamping their feet and breathing on their hands to keep warm. As they ticked off the beads on the abacus, they periodically looked up outside at the street vendors, who recoiled the neck with cold and hawked the steamed cakes, sheep blood soup, things for stitchery, hats and scarfs. The street barber carried the shoulder pole that, as commonly described, sticking up at the two ends, one end hung with the wind-whipped stool and the other the stove used for heating up water for washing.

The horse drawn carriage, with large rubber wheels, ran the daily routine service, carrying passengers from the north suburb to downtown. The whisker being covered with icy scraps caused by breathing and freezing, the driver ate two bowls of dumpling soup and then asked the store assistant to send another bowl of it without pepper to a certain place at the Lane

The Temple of Kaiyuan. It was built in the Kaiyuan Period of the Tang Dynasty (713 A.D.) and renovated in the Kaibao Period of the Song Dynasty (968 A.D.). It originally housed more than three thousand classical works in the edition of the Song Dynasty. In the first half of the twentieth century, prostitutes gathered here. The Temple of Kaiyuan lost its Buddhist dignity, and became a nickname for brothel.

of Baoji before dusk. Laughing to his customer, the store assistant said, "To Miss Wang again?!" In fact Miss Wang was the oldest and ugliest woman in that lane. The old carriage driver did not flush. He replied that, old as he was, what he aspired was just to take a cozy sleep at night. Then he strode out of the door without looking back.

Winter was a sluggish season for prostitutes. Only those ladies at the Brothel of Kaiyuansi, who came

A vender (in the 1940s)

from Suzhou and Yangzhou, were engaged, exclusively booked and regularly visited by influential political and business men. The rest of the women generally stayed idle in business. Those harlots at the Lane of Prosperity, the brothels with low-class women, could expect nothing but the patronage of carriage drivers, venders and hawkers, and their service was as cheap as the cost of one bowl of warm dumpling soup.

Probably kids found winter the most enjoyable time of the year. They fought snowball battles on the lane and street, shot slingshots on the icicles hanging under the eaves of some households, and stuffed the chimneys of the heatable bed of some families with brick fragments and weeds. They sweated on the head, though blood oozed from the cracks of their hands and

A little girl clad in the long slit skirt with the "Turtle Braid" fixed on top of the head.

feet with cold. The hairdo of children did not vary from city to country. The hair, hung in the rectangular shape across the forehead, is called the horse's mane style, or a strand of hair grew at the back of the head like the peacock tail. On top of the head another strand of hair, called the head-hair style, linked the rectangular hair in the front and the peacock tail at the back. The kids usually wore an iron ring around the neck, fastened with the Eight Diagrams copper coin and the 24-star copper coin that jingled incessantly in walks.

Sometimes boys and girls got wild. They would run all the way to the Camel Alley at the Western Gate to watch street scenes. Leading along tens of camels

A young child wearing a tiger hat in the winter

carrying the raw salt on the back, the merchants came from Gansu, Ningxie and Qinghai, wearing the long sheepskin-lined overcoat without the outside covering. They pitched tents and took rest, as the camels lay on their legs outside the tent. The children were interested not in the men drinking wine in large bowls and women singing the song of "Flower" inside the tent, nor in the camels' amusing gallop seen from behind. The kids found fun in watching the camels lying there chewing forage with the mouth covered up with a cotton bag.

A caravan of camels at recess

A street folk art performance in Xi'an in the 1930s

Eulogy and Infuriation

Shaanxi is an inland province. Most of the people have never seen the sea. In the desert to the north people there call a little pond the see. Admittedly people from Xi'an also regard the character "sea" as referring to something massive. For example, when describing a high-ranking official, they say, "He has had an official career as large as the sea!" A large bowl is also called a "sea bowl". The sea bowl is used in all the restaurants serving steamed buns soaked in mutton soup and noodles.

Li Si, prime minister of the Qin Dynasty (221-206 B.C.), for the unification of language, assigned the language used in the State of Qin as the offi-

A sea bowl

A band of Chinese
woodwind horn on the
outskirts of Xi'an

cial language of the country. But in 1949 when the new
China started practicing Mandarin, the Xi'an dialect
was reduced to the intolerance of alien accent. Theo-
retically the Xi'an dialect is under the same linguistic
system with other northern languages, and people from
Xi'an should have had no problem speaking Mandarin.
The reality proves the opposite is true. The difficulties
they have in pronunciation stem in part from the many
falling tones, stresses and unclear utterances in their
local dialect.

Another reason for the pronunciation problem re-
sides in the megalomania and conservatism of the
dialect. However, this conservatism has helped pre-
serve the Xi'an dialect with a fair amount of China's
ancient language in the form of vernacular. I once collected a great deal of Xi'an local expressions that de-

Probably this character cannot be found in any dictionary throughout the Chinese history. It is pronounced "bia".

rive from the language of antique, and discovered the verb takes the largest proportion of the vocabulary. I also studied and traced the original meanings in ancient times of some popular set phrases and words. This study benefits me a lot in terms of literary writing. Many writers and readers are impressed by my mastery of classical Chinese. Actually they flatter and don't quite understand me. What I have done is only understanding the features of the Xi'an dialect and absorbing some things from the local folk language.

I have lived in this city for nearly three decades. I am proud of myself having the opportunity of staying in a city of profound civilization and pursuing my writing career. I am physically fragile but take pleasure in ascending the city wall once a month and strolling outside the south gate. Those moments often fill me with rising confidence and a feeling of being somebody. Naturally I have acquired the annoying defects that people from Xi'an have. For example, they are introversive. But, to a more degree, at times they feel the desire to air their mind, they are the most arrogant, and, at times of adversity, they are the most

The towers on the East Gate in Xi'an (1936)

A few foreign missionaries occasionally seen in Xi'an toward the end of the Qing Dynasty

disillusioned. In Chang'an, the capital city of the Tang Dynasty, as portrayed in historical books and frescoes handed down, ordinary people are tall and sturdy, casually dressed and carefree. Learned men, not restrained by rituals, behave unconventionally, like Li Ba who gets drunk, laughs wildly and lies down in the tavern, ignoring the emperor's arrival by refusing to get on board a boat and leave. In Chang'an in the Tan Dynasty, the young Huo Qubing leads his troops in

The Pond of Huaqing in Xian at the beginning of the twentieth century

The Pond of Huaqing (1930)

west military expeditions and sweeps away all enemies. He pours the wine, granted him by the emperor, into the well so that his officers and soldiers can share gulps of it. What a thrilling scene!

Starting from the Ming and Qin Dynasties, Shaanxi was on a gradual decline. Now it is still a city on the perimeter. People of Xi'an have a strong aspiration for revival, because the supreme civilization keeps pounding on their heart for change. For many years efforts have been spared in searching for reasons for its fall.

A horse-fastening stake

Numerous symposiums have been held, and loud chants of restoring to the city the prosperity and power of the Han and Tang Dynasties have repeatedly sounded across the country. But the dream of making a strong northwest city with a pivotal role in the country still has not come true.

A stone lion at Yulin

I wrote a few articles and put forward my viewpoints. I think there are six reasons that have held Xi'an in check for development today. A shortage of water resource definitely hinders the growth of a city. In Chinese history thirty-six states died out in the northwest because of the cut-off of the water source and the erosion of desert. In ancient time Xi'an was surrounded by eight rivers. Today all but the Jing and Wei Rivers are either completely dry or wrecked with a minimum flow of water. The scarcity of water even affects the use of drinking water in the city of today, and a canal has to be built drawing water from the Hei River at the foot of Mount Taibai. This is the first reason.

Transportation is the artery of the economy. An inland province, Shaanxi is crippled by a limited highway system. Though quite a number of railways and highways have been built centering around Xi'an in recent years, a highly developed transportation system radiating to its vicinity remains a dream to have. This is the second reason. People from Xi'an are constantly influenced by the prevailing, tacitly approved idea that the country's political, economic and cultural gravity is moving north and east. This is the third reason.

The above three reasons give rise to the fourth that foreign influences did not reach Xi'an in the Ming and Qing Dynasties, a good fortune to be rejoiced with at that time. But the city was deprived of the opportunities for embracing advanced ideas of business. The practice of relying on the laurels the city enjoyed in

A Muslim school student holding a cow-bone book in his hands

history, inhibits the imagination and creativity of the people, which constitutes the fifth reason. The sixth reason comes from the indolence and content that have been gradually shaped among the people. Such lack of dedication in character is an outgrowth of large numbers of nomadic tribes and homeless people entering the city, the former being satisfied with small business profits and the latter more disorganized and socially devastating. Chang'an, despite its long history of stability, has eventually been dispossessed of its ambition and vigor.

I will digress to talk a little more about the history. There is a place, called Zhidaoting, to the east of Chanan of the Han Dynasty, in which military guards were stationed to examine the passers-by. One night the famous military general Li Guang passed this place. The officer on duty was Ba Lingwei, who was drunk and

The Jing Canal (a dam)

became abnormally strict with regulations. He stopped Li Guang and, ignoring Li's followers explaining of the general's identity, put him in custody for one night on the excuse of the rule enforcement. Later when Li Guang was on a military expedition, he, with the power granted by the emperor, purposely picked up this Ba Lingwei for joining his troops and executed him as soon as the latter complied.

The poet Li Bai was in the favor of the emperor and respected in all parts of the country. Many government officials vied with one another to buy over the manager of tavern in a hope to meet the poet and ask him to write a poem or put in a few good words in front of the emperor. When out of favor and sent on

The Xi'an railway station on the railway line from Shanghai to Lanzhou.

a tour of exile, Li Bai found himself alone and shunted in departure. He was a great drinker. At the moment of leaving, he hoped to drink once more the wine fermented with osmanthus flowers. The keeper of the Tavern of Drinking More was reluctant to meet him and asked his men to slight him with the wine mixed with water.

The isolation and content has gradually toned down Xi'an to a place of neglect, and many gifted people have left for other parts of the country. It is said that, since the country's economic reform and opening to the world, Xi'an has become the city that has lost the largest number of talents in the country.

This section of the Great Wall, built in the Ming Dynasty, is the best preserved of all and one of the largest and most completely protected ancient military fortifications in the world.

The city wall and tower of Xi'an, built in the Ming Dynasty, with a history of six hundred years.

After the death of Yang the Highest-ranking Imperial Concubine, "whose beauty eclipses all young ladies throughout the whole imperial court," the emperor Xuanzong became overwhelmed with grief, when staying for the night at an inn on his flight to western Sichuan and hearing, in his dream, Yang's calling "Third Brother" to him in the company of the Aeolian bells. The residents of Chang'an were all eagerly in going to her tomb at Maweipo, getting a handful of earth from the tomb and bringing it back home for gardening, believing plants would grow in exuberance with the earth. Because of this the tomb was leveled later. It was rebuilt and leveled again.

Sima Qian made candid suggestions to the emperor Wudi and received the penalty of castration. His descendants added one vertical stroke on the left side of the character of Si to make it the character of Tong and two slanting strokes on the left side of the character of Ma to make it the character of Feng, not so be-

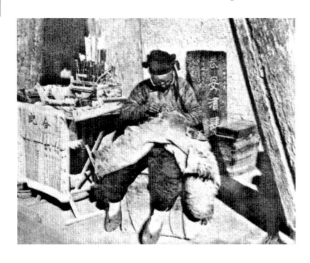

The Taoist fortune-teller is sewing on his own Taoist robe, truly a self-service.

A large-wheeled cow-drawn cart on the suburbs of Xi'an (1936). The huge wooden wheels roll easily on the ground of loess.

cause they were afraid of their entire family being exterminated as because they felt humiliated.

It is commonly believed that Jingke deserves condemnation from the people of Shaanxi for his unsuccessful assassination of the emperor of the Qin. But in the following dynasties, the First Emperor of the Qin Dynasty has been despised as a tyrant. So the tomb of

A singing girl performs in a little tea house around the corner of street in Xi'an

Jingke was built in the city of Xi'an and has been protected so far. As for the tomb of Dong Zhongshu, it is said to be somewhere around town, in the southern part of the city one moment and the northern part of it the next. A few years ago his tombstone was found by the latrines in a compound accommodating many households. But no tomb was built for him.

When Cixi the Dowager fled to Xi'an, it was a most critical juncture for the country. A man, surnamed Shi, bribed Li Lianying, in an attempt to obtain a promotion to the position of prefecture head. Shockingly the Dowager uttered, "I'm now in danger, away from home. So the cost for it can be lowered. However, the promotion to prefecture head is two ranks higher. It takes at least ten thousand silver coins." Soon getting promotion and official titles through bribery became a common practice in the capital city. When the "Representative Conference of the Kuomingtang central government" was being held in 1947, the important persons in Xi'an went into the race for representative positions,

During the dry season the Bridge of Ba becomes a scenic spot.

The tomb of Yang the Highest-ranking Imperial Concubine (719-756 A.D.) at Maweipo in the county of Xingping west of Xi'an. Though she is one of the most beautiful concubines in Chinese history, her tomb is simple and unadorned. She was the most favored concubine of the emperor Xuanzong (reigning in 712-756 A.D.) of the Tang Dynasty. In 755 a revolt broke out in the imperial court. She fled west and was forced to suicide on her arrival at Maweipo.

and the poster was seen everywhere on the street, "Please vote for so and so." A man, surnamed Ma, even hired a truck to stop at one corner of the street, calling out, "One bowl of mutton soup with steamed buns for one vote!" and hailing pedestrians to get on the truck for the dinner at a restaurant.

In his late years, Liu Qing suffered from pulmonary emphysema. He wore a long Chinese-style gown with buttons down the right side and was bare-headed. He had a bad cough, which often threatened his life. When he had to take the crowded bus, no one showed courtesy to him by letting him go through so he had to crawl between legs to get off the bus. Shi Lu, during the Cultural Revolution, went insane after the mass sessions of criticism and abuse. He went to the meat market and stood in line. People bought pork but he wanted the gall bladder. The customers knew it was Shi Lu but laughed at him and pushed him out of the line. Such and other anecdotes humiliate Xi'an, which gradually loses its grip on its intellectuals. A great number of talented people grow and live in the city to be unknown in life. But they stun the world with their achievements in other parts of the country. Xi'an has suffered the greatest outflow of accomplished persons in the past twenty years, as lamented in the call of the poetic line, "Peacocks fly southeast." He Haixia, a noted painter of traditional Chinese painting, wrote in the elegiac couplet to Shi Lu, "People are raised in and leave Xi'an, but a resting place does not have to be Xi'an." Later he himself left Xi'an too.

The tomb of the noble Jingke. In 227 B.C., the crown prince of the State of Yan sent Jingke to assassinate the emperor Yingzheng of the State of Qing (namely the First Emperor of the Qing Dynasty). But Jingke missed his target in the action and was killed instead. Supposedly people of Shaanxi would have hated Jingke. However, his tomb has been protected inside Xi'an.

Tall and verdant ancient trees provide shady areas across the yard of the Temple of Learning.

Chapter 3
A Land of Culture
and A Source
of Intellectuality

The magnificent tower on the city wall

A distant view of the Large Tower of Wild Goose in Xi'an

Basked in Cultural Elegance

If all the scholars that have grown up or lived in Xi'an are taken into consideration, a complete history of Chinese literature can be written. "Inscribe one's name at the Large Tower of Wild Goose" was a popular saying in the Tang Dynasty, describing the scholars who won the position of taking the examinations on the imperial court and had dinner at Qujiang by the tower. Nobles and wealthy people also arrived with their family members to select son-in-laws among the young scholars. In one session of the Large Tower of Wild Goose meeting, the Tang's poet Bai Juyi wrote the line "At a tower of benevolence the inscription is written; among the seventeen scholars, I am taking the most spotlight."

I will leave out the scholars' lapse and dissolution,

A photo of the Northwest Opera the "Battle at Puguan" (1946)

committed after their success, and call attention to Xi'an's deep tradition of stressing the importance of culture and the respect to learning. I have been to many ordinary families and found them equipped, in one way or another, with some books and paintings. For a few times I saw the two scrolls vertically hung in the living room with the characters written on it, "A top-notch person should be loyal to the emperor and filial to his parents; two things to be done in life are reading and farming," and "Reading brings one good fortune, and learning makes one better off." After having traveled around the country, I find the stores in Xi'an the most that have the horizontal boards with inscriptions of different styles of handwriting. Those stores include stalls and vending businesses of snacks like steamed cake, steamed pork and the cooled reed-leave-wrapped dumpling of glutinous rice and honey. Any small sign, stuck around the street corner, bears

Another photo taken in the 1940s of the Northwest Opera

the inscription of ancient well known writers.

Xi'an ranks third in the country in the number of colleges and universities. In many places, advertisements for programs of children's calligraphy, painting, vocal music and dance are conveniently seen on doors and gates. The popularity of the Northwest Opera is

inconceivable to one from another part of the country. At any informal performance, a dinner party or an evening gathering for cooling off, one can sing a few lines of the opera without hesitation, when the rest of the crowd join in the singing. On occasions of weddings and funerals, music professionals are hired to play through the ceremony. When a literary lecture is held, professional writers and amateurs arrive in large

A scene of the South Street after its completion of construction, the Xijing Department Store of Domestic Goods to the right.

numbers. If a famous author autographs his book for sale promotion at a bookstore, a few police officers have to come to help keep order. Societies for calligraphy and painting are too many for professionals to keep track of them.

Located in the county of Baishui not far from Xi'an,

In the 1930s the central section of the city wall was being built without the tower. So it was not considered as a city gate in Xi'an.

there is a place, the Temple of Cangjie, which is the birth place of the Chinese language. Stories about Canjie's creation of the language is various among the people. Great numbers of rubbings or even photos of the stone tablets in the Temple of Cangjie are bought and collected by the people of Xi'an. Three years ago, a red slip of paper appeared on the mud wall on the Street of Xiangzimiao to the west of the south gate, on which the characters were written, "Please value paper sheets written with characters to show virtue." Puzzled, I asked people around and got to know an old man.

Sitting in a restaurant of steamed buns soaked in mutton soup and breaking the bun into pieces, the man told me that when he was young the temples and Taoist shrines in Xi'an all had the iron stove set up inside them. Everyday monks and Taoists on duty were sent to go on the streets and lanes, shouldering the bamboo basket and holding in hand a long stick fastened with the nail at one end of it, and collect paper sheets written with characters. The sheets were brought back to the temple and burned inside the stove. At that time the characters were often written on the wall saying, "Characters are created by immortals and should be valued by everyone. If a scholar abuses characters and paper sheets written with them, misfortune will befall him by way of the Star of Learning and Music. He will be blocked from entering school and fail in examination. If the misconduct comes from a common person, he or she will go blind and stupid.

The ruins of the Pavilion of Tianlu. It was built in memory of the famous scholar Liu Xiang (206-25 B.C.), who sorted out research materials and wrote books here.

Shao Yuanchong and his wife pose with a Taoist.

Those who collect paper sheets written with characters will show boundless merits and virtues and live a
long fortune-blessed life." Xi'an is such a place that
worships learning that the people of Xi'an today would
have never tolerated the atrocity committed by the First
Emperor of the Qin Dynasty, who burned books and
buried alive learned men in pits.

A view of the out-
side of the meeting
place in Xi'an

In the Ming and Qing Dynasties a few well learned
scholars emerged in Xi'an, who established the Central Shaanxi Academy of Classical Learning. Today the
academy becomes a street name, and some of its buildings are preserved around the corner of the street. One
of the major learned scholars in the academy was Feng
Congwu who had the purpose for running the academy,
"Reading should be done to cover all areas and things
in the universe, and writing should be composed to
show earnestness and conscientiousness." In talking
about current affairs, he criticized crafty and corrupt
court officials. His lectures often drew an audience of
thousands.

The Central Shaanxi Academy of Classical Learning became the top institution of higher learning in Shaanxi in the Ming and Qing Dynasties, in which many scholars, including Number One Scholar Wang Duo and that scholar mentioned earlier, Zhao Shuqiao, were educated in their early years of career. At the beginning of the Qing Dynasty another well accomplished scholar appeared in Xi'an. It was Li Yong who, also a major lecturer at the academy, made contributions of far-reaching influence to the education of useful people and cultivation of good social practices in the province.

In contrast to scholars' pursuit of learning, ordinary people enjoyed themselves in folk entertainment. Situated by the side of the north end of the Bridge of Sajin in the city, the Temple of Celebration contains buildings built on five separate earth terraces on the slope running from east to west. Since there are the South Terrace of Five on the Zhongnan Hill in the south of the city and the North Terrace of Five in the county of Yao, this place is called the West Terrace of Five. An

Xi'an Normal School is situated on the Street of the Academy of Learning, originally the seat of the Central Shaanxi Academy of Classical Learning, which later became the cradle of the northwest students movement.

Xi'an Women's Normal School, located on the Street of Assistant Prime Minister, has a unique architecture. Today it is Xi'an Number 89 Middle School.

annual traditional fair is held here each year from the seventeenth to the nineteenth in June by the lunar calendar. One of the important item on the fair's agenda is to hold the competition of ancient Chang'an traditional music. In the past there were many music societies in Xi'an. They were not professional in any sense, combining religious purposes and leisured pursuits on the basis of the individual accord. So the participation indicated a harmony between spiritual worship and self-entertainment.

The music societies generally split into two categories, the societies of percussion instruments including the drum, cymbal, large cymbal and gong and the societies of wind instruments including the reed pipe instrument, vertical bamboo pipe, vertical bamboo flute and horizontal bamboo flute. With the music score written in the characters that were created in the Song Dynasty and unfit for the standard Chinese, the players played and handed down the ancient traditional music of the country, particularly some of the widely ranged music repertoire of the Tang Dynasty

The Zhongnan Hill in Xi'an is towering and undulating.

that were once played at banquets and for entertainment in the imperial court. In the course of the fair, because the abbot of the temple was a nun, many of the commodities were children's toys and local snacks sold by venders. Therefore women and children from the town swarmed to the fair, incense burned profusely and the place bustling in excitement and hubbub. Today some of the music societies have survived. Since the 1980s the Xi'an Art Festival of Ancient Chang'an Culture has been held each year, on which the ancient music, played by the popular music societies, has been placed in honor at the end of the performance.

If one visits the Museum of Chang'an Drum Music in the village of Hejiaying in the county of Chang'an, one sees on display there the drums used by the societies in various places and hundreds of music books and 40-odd pieces of the ancient music. Talking about the ancient music reminds me of Xun, an egg-shaped and six-holed wind instrument that was unearthed in the ruins at the Banpo Village. The sound produced by playing on Xun is muffled, loud and raucous. One evening we a few friends climbed to the top of the city

A view of the street in Xi'an (1934)

The ancient music instruments and books kept in the village of Hejiaying in the county of Changan

wall, carrying with us the instrument of Xun, and played it there. The simple vigorous melody touched a penetrating note of mystery, drawing crowds of people at the foot of the city wall. Some young ladies were even moved to tears. Xun is the best music instrument in expressing the Chinese national character and associating with Xi'an's richness in ancient culture. Today Xun is played in evening performances of various types in the city. It is usually a gourd-shaped instrument of fist size. The huge Xun is called Lu, like a water vat, which is placed on the pottery-making hill in the villages of matriarchal tribes at Banpo. No one is able to blow it except the heavenly wind.

Now it is time to talk about the art of Chinese chess in the city. In Xi'an Chinese chess is always more valued and popular than go. As northerners love gold and southerners like jewelry, Chinese chess fits the character of the people from Xi'an for its straightforwardness, intense conflict and simplicity. Players can play games at home and on the street. But the best place for playing is always at the tea house. The well known chess-playing tea houses in the old Xi'an are the Mao's Tea House at the Fair of Horse and Mule, the Tea Hall of Good and Loyalty at the People's Market in the southeast of the city, and the Zhang's Tea Hall and the Zhen's Tea House in the northeast of the city. In the years between the end of the Qing Dynasty and the founding of the new China, capable players of the city raised challenge, over a wooden chess board of jujube tree that was usually placed outside the door of these tea houses, to players all over the city. Players signed up for games and spectators came in flocks. When a major competition was held, a large

A tea house in Xian of the past, in which men chat, drink tea and while away the time.

master chess board had to be hung up, and deck chairs and long benches were all occupied. Hundreds of people were content with standing and watching the game, the tea pot supported in hand. The running of the competitions in those years gave rise to many good players. Only in the Mao's Tea House alone, five top players were selected by polls. The top one of them was a man called Zhao Shuanzhu, who made a living by selling cigarettes and melon seeds and was known for his quick, fierce and devastating style of playing.

A "Sparks" advertisement from the Xian Match Factory of the China's Industrial Corporation. Today the "Sparks" advertisement can only be seen in the collector's home.

In the early spring 1949, after many years of disappearing, Zhao suddenly emerged in the Mao's Tea House, humpbacked and completely gray-haired. Word got around quickly throughout the town: the top player has been back again! On the day that he played games of challenge to others, the tea house was packed to the ceiling. Spectators standing in the outer rings of the crowds could not see the chess board, when outcries of surprise, praise and acclaim kept rising from inside. His opponents admitted defeat one after another until the evening when no one dared to take up the gauntlet. Sitting cross-legged on the rush cushion, Zhao Shuanzhu stroked the wooden pieces of jujube tree, tears rolling down his year-seasoned cheeks. The following day when chess funs came back to the tea house, with a long horizontal inscribed board, to give him the title of Chang'an Chess Master, they found the old man gone at midnight. He was never heard again.

Now I have to turn to the Northwest Opera. In

talking about the opera, how can one avoid mentioning the Society of Custom Transformation? In his reign (712-756 A.D.) the emperor Xuanzong of the Tang Dynasty showed, through his life in the Palace of Long Peace, that he was a great patron of theater. He loved women but art even more. Not only did he write plays and dances to perform together with Yang the Highest-ranking Imperial Concubine, he established an institution specially designed for training players of popular music. The players rehearsed at the Garden of Pear. Later the Garden of Pear became a synonym for opera. In the Tang Dynasty, the Garden of Pear was situated in the village of white poplar of today on the north outskirts of the city. In Xi'an the Circle of Garden of Pear was founded at the Fair of Horse and Mule two hundred years ago.

With the long theatrical tradition, societies of the opera have remained flourishing

A stage photo of the Northwest Opera (1942)

The Xi'an's post office building

A view of the south-
ern avenue in its early
years

The great scholar
on classical Chinese Lu
Xun

throughout ages and produced many outstanding
players. Ordinary people listen to and watch plays
and, to a large degree, take singing opera arias as an
integral part of their life. There is a story about a military man who was pulled up to the guillotine for violat-
ing the military code of conduct. All of a sudden, he
broke into the indignant roar of a song from the Northwest Opera. Admiring his gallantry, the commander
remitted the execution and he was back to life.

During the Revolution of 1911, revolutionary intellectuals in Xi'an set up the Society of Custom
Transformation, Society of Three Ideas, Society of
Hazel and Reed, and Society of Custom Redress, writing and performing new operas on the basis of democratic ideas in an effort to combine education and
entertainment, enlighten the populace, change prevailing habits and transform customs. Among them the
Society of Custom Transformation was the most
successful. In the summer 1924 Lu Xun came to Xi'an

with other ten professors on a lecture tour and made a special visit to the Society for watching the opera. A southerner, Lu Xun could not understand the singing so he asked a man from Shaoxing, his home town, to interpret for him. He said, "Though the words are hard on me, the story, the performance, and, particularly, the songs of the play are wonderful." In his stay of less than twenty days in the city, he made five calls for watching the opera and wrote the inscription "Ancient Songs and Unique Music" to the Society.

At that time the most popular player of the Society was the female role actor Liu Zhensu. In 1921 when the Society went to Hankou for performance, it happened that the Nantong Academy of Theater headed by Ouyang Yuqian was putting on plays there too. Ouyang Yuqian spoke highly of Liu's performing skills, saying, "I particularly like Liu Zhensu. He is indeed a talented actor, with a slender figure and a less than ordinary appearance. But, as soon as he stepped on the stage, I found him filled with tremendous potentials."

The play-watching crowds by a big tree

Later Liu dedicated great efforts to rehearsing and putting on the plays "Butterfly Cup," "Obtaining the Chamber," and "Xishi in Bathing. For a while his arts were assessed in the same breath with those of Mei Langfang and Ouyang Yuqian, as indicated in the saying that went about in the country, "In theater Mei tops in the north, Ouyang in the south and Liu in the west." Soon after Lu Xun's watching at the Society of Custom Transformation and leaving for Beijing, Liu Zhensu once again starred the play "Beauty and Horse" that he played for Lu Xun. But this time when he stepped on the stage, he suddenly fell into a swoon. In the following days he remained bed-ridden until he died in December that year at 22. A young gifted theatrical actor dead young,the procession, on the day of his funeral, ran one kilometer.

The music performance staged by the Society of Traditional Chinese Music of the Xi'an Orphanage

The gate of the private residence of Yang Hucheng — Zhiyuan on the Street of Jiufu in Xi'an (1936)

Upholding Truth and Composing Criticism

People from Xi'an believe one can be successful by incorporating himself into heaven, earth and nature. More often than not, in a little tavern on a narrow alley, some people are seen slovenly dressed and sitting alone at the table, drinking wine. They are quiet, ignoring the kids running amuck around them on the street. They may look down and lick up the wine spilt on the table. But, in chatting with an acquaintance, they each brim with a sense of responsibility for the future of the country. Despite many years of declining in modern civilization, Xi'an has retained its concerns with state

A snapshot of Zhang Xueliang and Yang Hucheng taking recess in their accompanying of Chiang Kai-shek on his visit to Xi'an. While Chiang grins, Zhang and Yang are serious in expression, brooding a plot for "proposing with military force."

affairs. With little food to fill up their stomach, peasants in Shaanxi plow in the field. But, when they sit down for break, the topic of their chat might be about the current and next Secretary Generals of the United Nations.

One day three peasants came to my home, carrying with them Heluo, (a corn-flour noodles handy for carrying and storing). One of them, engaged in the study of astronomical phenomena, spread a long piece of white cloth on the floor, pointing to the heavenly bodies he had painted on it. Another one read in philosophy. He recited to me long paragraphs from the writings by Georg Hegel and Immanuel Kant and then criticized Ren Jiyu, one of the renowned Chinese phi-

Yang Hucheng, one of the two major leaders in the Xi'an Incident, in which military force was used to push Chiang Kai-shek for taking initiatives in fighting against Japanese invasion.

The scripture inscribed pillar in the Temple of Cow Head in Xi'an

A remnant dragon-coiling stone stake in the Temple of Fragrant Town in Xi'an

The Temple of Flower Tower (or the Temple of Reverent Celebration) in Xi'an, built in the Sui Dynasty and renovated in the Tang Dynasty. It is so called because of its bright-colored bricks.

losophers of the day. Next he settled down in a babble of his recessive thinking, embarrassing me on the verge of dozing off. The last one once contacted my a couple of week before by sending a few telegrams and writing long letters on a recent pattern of world development, to which I did not reply. This time he presented his comments on the policies of the country on current foreign affairs, using his understanding of The Arts of Wa.r.

People from Shaanxi are interested in politics. But politics requires deception. They do well with tricks in the local arena but find themselves repeatedly outwitted when outside of Shaanxi, because of their inadequate personality. As a result few of them succeeded

A four-wheeled cart drawn by two cows is used for carrying both goods and passengers.

A distant view of the Lishan Hill showing the unique landscape of villages, fields and farmers on the outskirts of Xi'an

in becoming important political figures in the modern history of China. Yu Youren tops the list of the very few that secured high-ranking positions. But he failed in his run for vice presidency of the Kuomingtang. After coming to power, the First Emperor of the Qing Dynasty sent some people to Lantian in search of a jade for making the imperial seal. They found a phoenix keeping coming back to perch on a place. So they dug there and obtained a precious jade. Later digging for jade to make the official seal became a common practice. However, in the following generations, Lantian had never yielded a jade that graced the local people with the official seal of a higher-ranking position. Now the people, ordinary and cadres of the provincial government alike, are satisfied with a string of keys

A village on the outskirts of Xi'an, which contains plenty of well protected historical sites.

A scene of happy village life: the donkey pushing a millstone, kids playing and the housewife drying the millet.

dangling around the waist. The key symbolizes power at home.

The thought of scholars suddenly came to my mind. In history one is called "one pen", or "an effective writer", if he or she is accomplished in the composition of poetry and prose. But today the reality is that the "pens" or "effective writers" are those who draw up speeches and reports for leaders of the Party and governments at all Levels in Xi'an or counties of Shaanxi. These writers are embarrassed for the role they play. In their political career they are regarded as scholars. But in literary circles they are treated as officials. Scholars are divided into two kinds in officialdom, one who is subservient and ingratiating oneself, and the other who, unyielding to power, stands firm in upholding truth and is relentless in composing critical writings. In an ancient inn I saw the materials recording the arrival of the emperor Qianlong (reigning in 1736-1796) on his tour of inspection to south China. The local officials not only made reports of administration to His Majesty and paid tribute with local products, but selected the scholars to write poems in singing

Chiang Weiguo, a son of Chiang Kai-shek, marries the daughter of the textile tycoon Shi Fenxia in Xi'an. But Chiang Kai-shek considered the city as a place of infamy so he refused to attend the wedding ceremony.

The Pass of Tong, with the strong fortification confronting the enemy in front and the torrential river at its back for defense. Its strategic role is described in the poetic line by Du Fu, "Only one soldier is deployed to defense the pass through the ages." It is imaginable that thousands of enemy soldiers were killed in battles of attacking the pass.

praises. Though it is probably hard to find such poets today, if this practice is handed down, the local government often summons a group of painters, upon the arrival of a very important person, to a guest house to paint pictures and write poems. Many interesting historical stories in this regard often indicate the morality and personality of the scholars concerned.

Li Yong from Xi'an, one of the three most well learned men in classical Chinese in the early years of the Qing Dynasty, repeatedly turned down the summons from the emperor Kangxi (reigning in 1662-1723). As the stalemate went on, he had a sick certificate written and sent to the imperial court. The provincial and county officials threatened to punish his doctors and neighbors and finally had him carried, from the county of Fuping to Chang'an, on the flat wooden bed. Still refusing to cave in, Li went on a five-day hunger strike, with a dagger tucked under his arm in a threat to suicide. Eventually the Shaanxi governor He Zhan had to send a report to the emperor asking for a revocation on the excuse of his sickness.

In the war years of the 1930s-40s, some learned people in Xi'an, though not Communists, conducted a number of meritorious deeds. The painter Zhao Wangyun rejected the request for painting a palm-size picture for the war-lord. He stood up against the temptation of the luxurious house and grand feasts and, if threatened with force, took refuge by fleeing west at night to Dunhuang. The famous Northwest Opera ac-

The old man Qi
Baishi at painting

tor Wang Tianmin went to Ningxia for performance. The head of the local war-lords Ma Hongkui desired to keep the actor with him, so as to perform for him, by promising to give him a compound and ten thousand silver yuan as gifts. But Wang Tianmin' resolve to return to Xi'an never wavered. The well known·playwrights Fan Zidong and Sun Yuren, all well established in literary writing, worked for decades on end in adapting old plays and composing new ones to promote democracy, patriotism and anti-imperialism. Their plays have become classics in the canons of the Northwest Opera and even modern Chinese drama. The scholar Wu Mi returned to Shaanxi, his native place, in his late years. When others took an opportunist stance in the fast changing political situation of the day, "following closely the trend," Wu showed no fear in saying, "It is absolutely wrong to criticize Confucius, because some of his words are correct." For this he paid dearly, when he received intensified persecution and then died on the cold mud bed in grief and indignation.

There was a newspaper, Shaanxi Daily of Industry and Commerce, which often carried articles revealing the corruptions and briberies of the provincial and local administrative governments and, particularly after the victory over Japan, opposing the civil war and calling for the release of Yang Hucheng. The newspaper was cracked down upon by the government institutions that sent secret agents to ban the selling of the newspaper at stalls and ordered the police department to send secret notices to businesses requesting the suspension of their subscription and running advertisements in the newspaper. Unable to subscribe to the newspaper, readers went to the newspaper's office to pick it up. When the post office withheld delivering the newspaper, the newspaper office gave the newspaper to bus drivers on the morning shift, asking them to deliver it to the readers

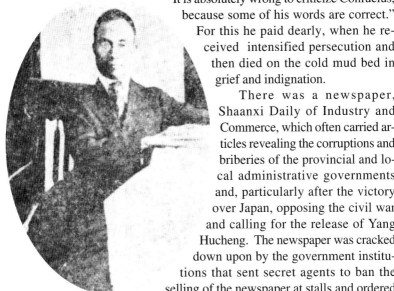

On January 25, 1927, Wu Mi, who taught at Hsing Hua University in Beijing, went to Xi'an to pay a visit to his father Wu Zhongqi and close friend Wu Fangji.

The postman hurries on with his journey day and night, lantern in hand, to deliver mail from Xi'an to Fengxiang. The dependence on walking for the work is inconceivable today.

along the railway and bus lines. Seeing their covert sabotage prove ineffective, the government institutions mustered a mob of gangsters and ravaged the business office of the newspaper and threatened to place incendiary time bomb and set on fire its printing house. They even sent the truck to knock down the editor-in-chief and break his legs. Some of the correspondents

The first postal van in Xi'an. It was something new at that time.

In 1942 the building of the Shaanxi Branch of the Postal Remittances and Savings Bank was completed. The branch office merged with the post office at the south gate, showing the progress of the postal service.

of the newspaper were closed in on at the dead end of the lane, and the pepper and lime were strewn over their eyes and mouths. The hardest blow came when the well known newspaper manager Li Furen was kidnapped, and the newspaper's founder Du Bincheng was assassinated.

Du Bincheng, a democratic patriot who comes from the county of Mizhi. In 1922 he got to know Yang Hucheng. Du established the newspaper Shaanxi Daily of Industry and Commerce. During the Xi'an Incident, he advocated the alliance with the Communist Party, opposition to Chiang Kaishek and resistance against Japanese aggression. Later he assumed the position of head secretary of the Shaanxi provincial government. He was assassinated on October 7, 1947.

The survey is being done on the slope when the renovation work is under way on the east avenue.

The Forever Vigorous Ancient Capital

I often ponder. What is a city? A heap of cement and crowds of people. When we ride the bike to go to work, we are annoyed by those people driving their private car zipping by and often getting in the bike route. When we can afford taking taxi or driving our own car, we are enraged by the bike pedalers who block the way. Everyone complains about the crowded life, noise and air pollution but no one wants to move out of town. During the day, traffic gets jammed and pedestrians edge in swarms. But when dusk falls, streets are deserted in solitary dim street lamplight. Street cleaners lethargically swang the broom with their hands across the surface of the road. Occasionally a few

Sightseers take a break on the Bridge of Bai, as willow trees wave in the breeze.

The city moat is no longer the defense.

The cow cart sails across the river (taken in the 1940s).

drunkards crop up from the night club, supporting each other, and reel toward home. You can't imagine where the people have gone. Why has no one lost his way? The streets of Xi'an are designed on a neatly parallel and crisscross outline, like the Chinese character "Jing", dignified and rigid. Today the names of shops are constantly reminiscent of the distant past. One's mind is immediately aroused to span to ancient times at the sight of the monks clad in the yellow, dark-grey colored long gown. But through the vicissitudes of the thousands of years, the city kept declining to the base. In the last fifty years since the founding of the new China, efforts have been made to reconstruct it. However, it is hardly possible to restore its past stately magnificence, given the remnants all over the impoverished imperial capital.

I firmly believe that a historical figure should be assessed on the contributions he made in bringing benefits to coming generations. In my judgment, the great

The west avenue before the renovation (It was paved with bricks later).

persons in Chinese history include the First Emperor of the Qin Dynasty, Wu Zetian, Sakyamuni, Lao-tzu, as well as others such as Huo Qubing and Sima Qian. A tour to the Museum of Terracotta in Lintong, the Tomb of the Emperor Qian, the Temple of Famen, the Tower of View, the Mausoleum of the Emperor Huangdi and Yanan would convince you that the towns, which possess these spots of historical interest associated with the historical figures, are bustling with hotels, restaurants and public houses of entertainment. In addition to the tremendous contributions the great people made to the development of China and enhancement of the country's reputation, the thriving tourism, as well as the revenue raked on the entrance ticket to the spots, is an outgrowth of the legacy. A city flourishes in the expansion of population, infrastructure, communications, industry, business corporations, banking, and maintenance of law and administration, among other factors. But the humanity of the society cannot advance without the line of ethic guidance. Therefore religion comes into being, and temples are built for the need.

A little girl with the dangling braid in front of an antique shop. Just be basked in the sunshine.

西安孤兒教養院高級小學校第二次畢業生院撮影·六、三

A photo of the graduation from an elementary school in Xi'an, taken on July 30, 1929. The eight-pointed hap is unique.

One of the important reasons that Xi'an deserves notice is its preservation of huge numbers of imperial tombs and religious temples, those underground and those on the ground, the legacy of national culture that keeps the city teeming with vigor and appeal. According to the historical records, at the site of Chang'an of the Tang Dynasty, there are 140 Buddhist temples and 41 Taoist temples. Among them the most well known include the Temple of Boundless Good, Temple of Immense Solemnity, Temple of Black Dragon, Temple of Sole Learning, Temple of Traveling Immortal, Temple of Longevity, Temple of Gratitude, Temple of Huayan, Temple of Grace, Temple of Ximing, Temple of

A view from on top of the tower on the west gate over the west avenue before its renovation.

The project on a road on the outskirts of Xi'an is near completion.

Fortune Showing, Temple of Wealth Rejection, Temple of Fragrance Gathering, Temple of Straw Shed, Temple of Sleeping Dragon, Temple of Buddhist Baptism, Terrace of Tower Watching, Palace of Chongyang, Shrine of Eight Immortals, Temple of East Mountain, the Grand Xi'an Mosque. The ten major Buddhist sects, except the sects of Tiantai and Chanzong, all originate in Xi'an. These temples are splendid with various multicolored frescoes, some of them showing figures of elegantly dressed graceful immortals and others didactic "pictures of the diabolical world." They supply many sources of legendary and fantastic tale for the populace. The story of *the Reunion of Husband and Wife* took place at the Temple of Ximing. The temple was originally the residence of Yang Su, Prince of Yueguo, in the last Tang and early Sui Dynasty. Later the place was confiscated by the state for Yang's involvement in the plot for rebellion. He was in power at that time. The third younger sister of the Emperor of the State Chen married low to Xu Deyan, a servant of the crown prince.

The Clock Tower of Xi'an (1937)

When the State of Chen was perishing under invasion, Xu said to his wife, "After our country is destroyed, we will not be able to stay together. You're beautiful and can surely be married into a family of imperial descent or nobility. We have loved each other and should

The busy traffic and crowds of people in front of the post office in Xi'an, a street scene in the 1940s.

The Little Tower of Wild Goose at the Temple of Fortune Showing

The Ming's Wen in the Temple of Learning in Xi'an. "Wen" is an important decoration on the ancient building. It is a dragon head of brick carved in this temple in the Ming Dynasty. The exquisite craftsmanship indicates a high style of aesthetics at that time.

This is the entrance of the Temple of Grace in 1936.

A stele with the inscription of the Buddhist scriptures and the signature of the emperor Xuanzong of the Tang Dynasty in the Forest of Steles in Xi'an.

remain forever faithful. I will break the mirror into two parts and each of us takes one. Let us schedule the meeting at the center of the town for selling the broken mirror on the fifteenth day of the first month by the lunar calendar in the next year. If the two parts come together, we will know the other is still alive. It turned out that his wife was indeed taken as concubine by Yang Su after the fall of the State Chen. Yang heaped favor on her. However, her heart was set on her husband. On the fifteenth day of the first month next year, she sent the girl servant to the town for selling her part of the mirror. As expected, the girl servant met Xu Deyan, who gave his part of the mirror and a poem to her. The poem read,

"Gone was the man with the broken mirror, and now the broken mirror returns with the man

A distant view on the Temple of Grace in Xi'an. It is said that the eminent monk Tang Xuanzang stayed here to translate seventy-four volumes, 1338 chapters, of the Buddhist scriptures.

Xi'an's water transportation (the postal boat) depends on the "northwest wind", so the sail is very large.

found nowhere. You are noble while I am still the man, My longing lingers painfully in the moonlight."

When the woman received the missing part of the mirror and the poem, she grieved so deeply that she went on fast. Then Yang Su heard the story. He was profoundly disturbed. After pondering for the whole night, he decided to send for Xu Deyan and return his wife to him.

Today the imperial tombs and ancient temples have become the cornerstone for the booming tourism in Xi'an. Gone is the peace and tranquility the city once knew. Occasionally a few monks and Taoists ramble down the street, plucking a note of antiquity and mysteriousness in the otherwise uneventful city life. Once in a while some of them, in threes or fours, with the beeper clipped around the waist, walk into a vegetarian restaurant for dinner, chatting and laughing broadly, drawing glimpses and stares of curiosity from city residents.

The wheelbarrows at the Little Tower of Wild Goose

A scene of the
Bridge of Chan in Xi'an

My Xi'an

One old saying goes "Barracks are stationary, while soldiers are on the move." It is true of the city, particularly a city like Xi'an. I made a survey on a large number of the city dwellers and discovered, surprisingly, that few of them are the descendants of the city residents five generations away. Farmers emigrate to this city and become city residents. A few generations later, their descendants move out of the city for some reasons, while new farmers come and settle down. It is a cycle of repetition. The present residents started living here in the 1920s and gradually developed prejudices against people from the countryside. So now they still oppose their child's marriage with someone who works in the city but has the rural background, in that the marriage will be burdened with financial responsibilities for and constantly disturbed by the family members of the other side from the country. Even with the parents all city residents, the child is still frown upon, for his or her Henan origin and growing up along the railway line outside of the North Gate, or the heavy nasal-sounded dialect and northern Shaanxi origin, despite the residential status. These people are looked on as being rough, careless and lack of family responsibility.

In fact the people of Henan origin are descendants of the refugees who fled Henan at times of flood. They become an important part of the city population. The people of northern Shaanxi origin are the offspring of the large number of revolutionary cadres that arrived with the Communist military troops from north China

Harvesting rice

A morning fair in the
countryside in Xi'an

Folk performances
in central Shaanxi

in the early years of the founding of the new China. These two kinds of people are hard-working, intelligent and capable of making a living and conducting political activities. The Xi'an population is primarily composed of the people from central Shaanxi, known for its vast fertile fields and better living conditions in comparison with other parts of the province. These people's conventional pride of living on a large plain grows into exclusiveness and helps shape their conservatism.

In my hometown Shangzhou, Xi'an was called the town at that time. Going to Xi'an was referred to as going to the town. In their early years, people of my father's generation walked for two weeks, carrying,

A well in a village in Xi'an. At times of drought it is precious and plays a vital role for the growth of crops.

An old couple living at the Temple of Huayan

on the shoulder pole, the tobacco, flaxen cords, paper for sacrifice and products of porcelain, and crossed over the Mountain Qinling to Xi'an for sale. Naturally it was hard to make profit on the sales. They often ended up in either working as assistants in the store or being gathered in a team to work in the coal mine in Tongguan, barely surviving on a meager life. But most of the time they went to work as wheat hands in harvesting the wheat in the suburbs of Xi'an in summer. Their typical attire was the gray down-buttoned Chinese jacket and a pair of straw sandals with a straw rope tied around the waist. They carried on their shoul-

城 南 小 雁 塔

The Little Tower of Wild Goose in the south of the city

der a cloth satchel with a bowl and parched flour in it. A sickle in hand, they toiled in the scorching sunshine, sweat streaming down the body. Sometimes the wheat hands arrived after the work started and could not find a job. Then they would huddle at the street corner or under the eaves of some household, drinking the rain when thirsty and eating the leftover in the restaurant when hungry. Their life was extremely harsh. Today in the countryside in China, wheat hands like them are

The "Northwest Lord" Hu Zongnan

occasionally seen in the harvest season of each year.

In the 1930s-40s drug-taking, gambling and prostitution were out of control. On occasions of the wedding or funeral, the rich family would cordially led the visitor into the room and onto the heatable bed, on which the smoking set was prepared. Most of the popular theatrical actors and actresses were opium addicted. Before the performance, they looked lean and haggard and kept yawning. But only a few draws refreshed them in high spirits, the face glowing with health. Many high-ranking political and military persons had their own drug and tobacco businesses. In terms of going to brothels, the rich and influential people in the political, military and financial circles were visitors to

The Bridge of Feng, built completely with stones, is situated across the Feng River between Xi'an and Xianyan.

Fenglingdu at the
Pass of Tong (1936)

The boatman at a ferry

those luxurious brothels at the Temple of Kaiyuan, which were guarded by soldiers at the entrance. It is said that Hu Zongnan was infected with the STD. I met an old deep-wrinkled prostitute. She was delighted, full of pride, in talking about her service to Hu Zongnan.

The city is a dwelling place for people. In such a place you can see all kinds of bird and encounter various unexpected events as far as your imagination can go. With a long history of ups and downs, the ancient capital Xi'an embodies affluence and poverty, civilization and ignorance, order and chaos, modernity and tradition. I have lived in Xi'an since 1972. Frankly

A distant view of the gorgeous Xi'an

speaking, I am no longer able to part from it. I sang the praises of it and cursed it. I had expectations from it and was upset by it. I will live the rest of my life here and become integral part of it, like a brick on the city wall or a street sign. As I come to the end of this book of random recollections of the city, I will have some final words to say, the words I have said thousands of times, "I love my Xi'an."

A group photo of fellow members of the Xi'an's Young Men's Christian Association

Shao Lizi, governor of the Shaanxi provincial government in the 1930s, poses with his friends at the "Garden of Vase".

Editors' Note

Changes a city has undergone are an important part of the history of the development of a civilization. In publishing this series of books, we have been guided by one consideration, i.e., to give readers a brief history of some well-known Chinese cities by looking at some old sepia photos taken there and reading some remembrances with regard to those cities.

Not like conventional publications, each book of this series contains a large number of old photos selected to form a pictorial commentary on the text. This provides a good possibility for readers to learn about Chinese urban history, cultural evolution in urban society in a new perspective. It also enables readers to re-experience historical "vicissitudes" of those cities and relish feelings of urban folks of China in the modern times.

To better illustrate those cities, we have commissioned renowned writers who have not only lived in their respective cities for a long time but also have been known for their strong local writing style. Either in presenting a panoramic view of a city or depicting fate of men in street, their writings are always so natural yet full of feelings.

This series of books have been published originally in Chinese by Jiangsu Fine Art Publishing House. The English edition has been published jointly by the Foreign Languages Press and Jiangsu Fine Art Publishing House.

Foreign Languages Press
Oct.2000 Beijing

图书在版编目(CIP)数据

老西安:废都斜阳:英文/贾平凹著 . —北京:外文出版社,2001
(老城市系列)
ISBN 7 - 119 - 02787 - 5
Ⅰ.老… Ⅱ.贾… Ⅲ.西安市 - 地方史 - 史料 - 英文Ⅳ.K294.11
中国版本图书馆 CIP 数据核字(2000)第 78797 号

中文原版

选题策划	叶兆言　何兆兴　顾华明　速　加
主　　编	朱成梁
副 主 编	何兆兴　郭必强　翟翠华
著　　文	贾平凹
图片供稿	中国第二历史档案馆
装帧设计	顾华明
责任编辑	速　加　何兆兴

英文版

策划编辑	兰佩瑾
翻　　译	马文谦
责任编辑	孙海玉

老西安·废都斜阳

©外文出版社
外文出版社出版
(中国北京百万庄大街 24 号)
邮政编码 100037
外文出版社网址:http://www.flp.com.cn
外文出版社电子信箱:info@flp.com.cn
　　　　　　　　sales@flp.com.cn
利丰雅高制作(深圳)有限公司印刷
2001 年(大 32 开)第 1 版
2001 年第 1 版第 1 次印刷
(英文)
ISBN 7 - 119 - 02787 - 5/J·1554(外)
08000(精)

OLD CITY